The Covid Beast

Why We Cannot Give Up Access to Our Bodies

Dr. Kevan D. Kruse, D.C.

Co Authors:
Dr. Dennis O'Hara, D.C.
and Alexandra Kruse

RIVER BIRCH PRESS

Daphne, Alabama

ISBN 978-1-956365-12-2 (print)
ISBN 978-1-956365-13-9 (e-book)
For Worldwide Distribution
Printed in the U.S.A.
River Birch Press
P.O. Box 868, Daphne, AL 36526

ii

Contents

Acknowledgments

I would like to thank Dr. Dennis O'Hara as a contributing author. Without his input and research into the Covid narrative, this book would not have been possible.

I also want to thank my wife, Alexandra, for putting up with me through this whole process. Not only am I thankful for her input, research, and editing, but I am also thankful that she helped me dialogue and formulate many of these ideas. Obviously, it is hard to live with someone constantly talking about conspiracy theories.

I also need to thank Dr. Anthony (Tony) Poncetti, Dr. Thomas Dozier, Gary Swink, and Pastor Rob Wren for their input, suggestions, and clarifications.

Introduction

Like many Americans, I have had a lot of difficulty trying to navigate through 2020 and 2021. But the most traumatizing part is that our country has changed into something I no longer recognize. Unfortunately, I have come to the conclusion that the most important hidden agenda of the Covid narrative is to gain access to our bodies whenever they want. This is a power no one but God should ever have. Consequently, the time has come to stand up and resist tyranny. After all, evil only wins when good people do nothing.

Unfortunately, most of us feel like there is nothing we can do. But if the twelve disciples of Jesus changed the world, then there is still hope for us. Unfortunately, we knew that the signature of the End Times would be deception, and that means lies upon lies. More importantly, finding the lies and who is telling them will help us recognize the agenda and who is in on it. The Bible is being fulfilled as we speak; unfortunately, the church is not sounding the alarm.

Consequently, I hope you will join me as we uncover a deception that is worthy of Satan and of being called the greatest of all time. I hope we can wake up a new generation to stop tyranny in its tracks. Lastly, I have been writing about Covid for over sixteen months, and there have been so many things happen it has been impossible to keep up with the new research that is coming out every day. Consequently, while I started at the beginning of the crisis, please realize that I have had to make updates as the narrative is still unraveling right in front of us.

1

Only Covid Lives Matter

The Purpose of Prophecy

For the testimony of Jesus is the spirit of prophecy (Revelation 19:10).

The purpose of Bible prophecy is not to predict the future. The purpose of Bible prophecy is to prove that God knows the future. Indeed, if God knows the future, then God knows our future. Most importantly, we can trust Him when He tells us that our future with Him is eternal and secure. The purpose of covering all of the prophetic portions of this book is to proclaim the testimony that Jesus is still Lord, even when Satan is the one making the headlines. The fact that God tells us these things in advance is supposed to give us peace. In a very real way, the spirit of prophecy is a form of encouragement.

I have told you these things, so that in me you may have peace. In this world you will have trouble. But take heart! I have overcome the world (John 16:33 NIV).

While there is some bad news about the trouble our enemy is causing, Jesus told us these things in advance that we might have hope. And not just hope, but something that lives inside our hearts that can bring heaven to earth. Whatever we are going through, God knew this was all going to happen. While this may be hard to hear, the troubles of this life are why life is a test of faith. Yet, faith is the currency of heaven and what God values the most. While we will be covering what Satan is doing, we do not want to miss out on what God is doing. Remember, God is building His eternal kingdom inside of us. We are the bricks of His expanding kingdom, and the Holy Spirit inside of us is the mortar holding us all together.

For we know that if the earthly tent we live in is destroyed, we have a building from God, an eternal house in heaven, not built by human hands (2 Corinthians 5:1 NIV).

What God is building inside of us cannot be made with human hands, but it can be enlarged in difficult times because the natural world can grow, test, and perfect our spiritual faith. Consequently, the message of this book is not one of gloom and doom, the message is that God is about to raise up a standard inside us all. God is going to come in like a flood and save a whole new generation (Isaiah 59:19). Just as Bible prophecy proved that Jesus was the Messiah, the Savior of the world, so too it proves that, once again, there is good news coming. More importantly, God is capable of doing something extraordinary inside of us to wake up a destiny that has been sleeping. We can all have a part to play in this divine drama, and it will be told for all eternity.

The Limitations of Prophecy

While Bible prophecy does talk about future events, it has more to do with God telling us what time it is, than it has to do with its predictive nature. Not only is prophecy cryptic, it is difficult to understand. We also need to keep in mind that if God gave too many specific details about the end times, Satan would just do the opposite. After all, even God doesn't want to give away all of His plans to the devil either. But there is a warning component to Bible prophecy that is designed to keep us from falling into enemy hands.

These warnings are meant to convey some immediacy because there is a tipping point before the fall. In times like these, I lean heavily on the Bible for my response. Indeed, my cipher and my attitude for interpreting Bible prophecy are found in Luke 21:28. "Now when these things begin to happen, look up and lift up your heads, because your redemption draws near." Reading all of Luke 21 reveals that before Jesus gives us this command, Jerusalem must no longer be trodden down by the gentiles. In other words, the Israelites must be in control of Jerusalem before we begin intensely focusing on the convergence between what is happening and what is in our Bibles.

In fact in 1967, Israel did take control of Jerusalem. This alone explains why much of Bible prophecy has been dormant for 2000 years, but now God's time clock is ticking again. The other implication is that our generation has become the target audience of what Jesus said in Luke 21:28. Careful study of the words reveals that the prophetic paradigm of Jesus does not need us to predict the future. But we are supposed to know when the prophetic parts of our Bibles are happening. The problem is the church isn't doing that or what Jesus says to do next.

We are specifically told to "stand up and lift up our heads." Standing up does not mean sitting down and being quiet. Unfortunately, our continued silence is also an acceptance. When pastors are silent, the flock assumes nothing important is happening. While we are commanded not to kneel, we are also told not to be discouraged either. Indeed, "while other men's hearts will be failing them for fear," our chins will be up because Jesus told us these things ahead of time so that we might have peace and not lose heart (John 16:33).

God is the one who is going to shake all the nations, and maybe that is because the church has fallen asleep. Yet, when we pretend nothing is happening or we stay silent, we insulate people from God's alarm system. Something has gone wrong when

Christians don't stand up or are overly discouraged by prophetic events. Unfortunately, preaching Bible prophecy has become synonymous with preaching fear instead of giving encouragement. In difficult times, prophecy tells us that God is still in control and that He has a plan for our lives.

Yet, somehow the church has fallen asleep and become so politically correct that it is failing to talk about the fact that our Bibles are happening. Sadly, church leaders have become afraid of Bible prophecy because the topics it addresses have become so controversial. Still, we must not fail to preach the whole of God's Word or put out a warning when what the Bible says is happening. We must not disregard the words of Jesus to "stand up and lift up our heads."

The difficult times we find ourselves in can help us realize our common denominator and recover our purpose to be salt in light of the decay around us. Remembering that God's kingdom is inside of us will also help us bring more of heaven to earth. In this sense, our hope is not delayed, God is here with us, and He is still working. Once again, God has called us to be His people and to stand up and look up for His kingdom.

All Lives Matter

Let's get right to it. The most startling part of COVID-19 narrative has been the disconnection between what we see on TV and a basic search for the facts. Before explaining further how only COVID-19 lives matter, I must first show that the total number of deaths, especially here in America, has been inflated and virtually manufactured. These are bold claims, but are they true?

Looking at two basic statements by the CDC, the Center for Disease Control, leads to this conclusion. The CDC would certainly be considered a good source for facts on Covid, so listen closely. The first evidence that something was amiss came when the CDC director agreed that hospitals have a monetary incentive to inflate COVID-19 data or deaths. He also said that increased numbers of specific diagnoses have already happened in the past with HIV/AIDS.

- https://www.christianpost.com/news/cdc-director-agrees-that-hospitals-have-monetary-incentive-to-inflate-covid-19-data-238244/?fbclid=IwAR0hgARG8YAAcWicIV0Sf pT5KniCCGZ3RvbE279TAYzqA4sRb1MoWAA7jA

- https://www.cspan.org/video/?c4897385/user-clip-cdc-director-acknowledges-inflation-covid-19-death-count

Unfortunately, there are lots of reasons why this inflation has happened. The first is that Covid shutdowns resulted in hospitals that were more than half empty. On top of that, all elective medical procedures were canceled. A billing specialist for multiple hospitals confirmed to me that billing was down 70-80%. Now, imagine that a Covid diagnosis pays more than anything else. Plus, there aren't even enough tests to confirm this diagnosis.

Maybe this is why it seemed that Covid was responsible for some new set of symptoms every day. Next, the validity of Covid testing has been questionable since day one. I had a nurse, who works in a contagious disease practice, say that they do not do Covid testing because there are no accurate tests. I also had many nurses tell me that they tested positive and negative off and on for three months. To make matters worse, several of my patients received COVID-19 test results when they were never even tested.

These instances are why we all know they have been diagnosing people with Covid, even though it was a car accident. In addition, I have had patients report that the hospital asked the family if they could list Covid-19 as the cause of death. One family was even offered $5000. These stories explain why routine audits of Covid deaths have somewhere between 30-50% inaccuracy. Here is one such article on the inaccuracy of Covid deaths, including deaths that had already been counted.

- https://www.tri-cityherald.com/news/coronavirus/article246326410.html

The next piece of information that causes us to question the Covid numbers happened when the CDC released the fact that 94% of COVID-19 deaths had underlying conditions, while only 6% died of the virus alone. My first question was, if there was an underlying condition, then why did they diagnose them with Covid at all? Usually, the underlying condition is listed as the cause of death, not an "active" or "immediate" condition. Unfortunately, we already answered why. Money. Furthermore, the CDC issued a guidance change in how death certificates were done. In other words, they changed how they counted the deaths right before this all started.

The 94% represents the CDC being truthful about how the deaths would have been counted previously without this guidance change. Unfortunately, they did not say what these underlying conditions were, which would have been helpful to come up with differential prognoses relative to the risk level of each individual. Unfortunately, we have reverted to a one size fits all for Covid, which is based upon the worst patient scenario and not the best. Lack of following standard medical procedures has caused us to treat those who have 0% risk with 100% fear, 100% of the time. This lack of clarity has caused us to try and force treatments on patients that have no risk of dying and will not be harmed in any way by catching Covid. So, why are they trying to scare everyone? What do they have to gain, and what is the hidden agenda?

- https://www.christianpost.com/news/94-of-covid-19-deaths-had-underlying-health-problems-6-died-of-virus-alone-cdc-238680/?fbclid=IwAR0LkPG-WoKNBkm0pFEiF0U5r9DwTT4TM_5PLqafJhqf2MzWbpN9lb9nekQ

The Price of a Life

Yet the larger question is how do the Covid deaths factor into other mortality figures? Indeed, death is scary enough without someone giving 24 /7 coverage of it. So the question is, "What deaths are we not being told about that will that add some much-needed perspective?" Unfortunately, not all lives are valued the same. The following statistics reveal a startling truth, "Only Covid lives matter."

According to the international relief agency Mercy Corps, 9 million people die of hunger each year. That's more than the death toll of AIDS, malaria, and tuberculosis combined. Just as important is that Covid shutdowns may end up doubling the number of deaths due to hunger. Look at the increase in the cost of food since Covid. Food prices have gone up close to 30%. Amazingly, we could end world hunger for 256 billion per year.

- https://www.globalgiving.org/learn/how-much-would-it-cost-to-end-world-hunger/

- https://www.npr.org/sections/coronavirus-live-up-dates/2020/05/05/850470436/u-n-warns-number-of-people-starving-to-death-could-double-amid-pandemic

Malaria is also a disease that is somewhat easily fixed. According to the World Health Organization, more than a million people in Africa die from malaria every year, including 3,000 children each day. We could fix this problem for about 2 million dollars. The average cost of treating an episode of uncomplicated malaria was only $5.84. Some more severe cases could average up to $30.26. If 10% of the cases are severe, then this would be less than 9 million dollars to treat the majority of malaria cases.

- https://earthdata.nasa.gov/learn/sensing-our planet/malaria-by-the-numbers

- https://malariajournal.biomedcentral.com/articles/
  10.1186/1475-2875-10-337

The last type of unnecessary deaths we will talk about have to do with waterborne illnesses. Every year 3,575,000 people die from drinking contaminated water, most of which are children. According to the *New York Times*, we could provide clean water to everyone on the planet for about $10 billion. In total, ending world hunger, malaria, and waterborne illnesses would save 12.575 million lives per year.

- https://www.theworldcounts.com/challenges/planet-
  earth/freshwater/deaths-from-dirty-water/story

Only "Covid-19 lives matter" even though there are many more significant killers that have shockingly cost-effective and straightforward solutions. Now follow the money. We have initially spent more than 6.5 trillion dollars just on a stimulus package to shut things down for 12 weeks. But suppose we add in the 6.5 trillion 2020 government spending on Covid, the 2020 deficit of $3.1 trillion, stimulus spending of $2.6 trillion, stimulus tax relief of $900 billion, and a second stimulus proposal of approximately $2 trillion. In that case, we come to a grand total of about 15.1 trillion.

Five Breathtaking Numbers Reveal the Unsettling Cost of Stimulus

- https://www.forbes.com/sites/robertberger/2020/10/18/5-
  big-numbers-reveal-the-unsettling-scope-of-stimulus-
  spending/?sh=35ecf10b142b

To make matters worse, we haven't even considered the future impact of our decisions. The growing federal deficit alone tells us we are an insolvent country. We are resting on our past as if it carries any prowess in the future. Either way, this was a massive amount of money to spend essentially to delay the COVID-19 phenomenon for a few weeks.

Now let's do some math. We have spent 15.1 trillion dollars just to slow down Covid in America. According to the CDC, during the first 18 months, 375,000 people died of Covid in the US even though the deaths were counted differently than previous years, and the numbers have been incentivized.

- For $256 billion we could have saved 9 million lives due to hunger.

- For $10 billion, we could have saved 3.57 million lives due to contaminated water.

- For around $9 million, we could save about one million lives from malaria.

- In total, we could have saved 13.57 million people for approximately $267 billion.

- Divide this number by $15.1 trillion, and we realize that for about 1.8% of the money we spent on Covid, we could have saved 36 times as many people.

Now let the insanity of that sink in. If these deaths aren't scary enough, the Guttmacher Institute estimates that in 2017 the abortions in America reached 862,320. Compare this to the 375,000 Covid deaths of 2020, and we can see that abortions are close to three times as many deaths as Covid. Why don't babies' lives matter? What is becoming painfully obvious is that only certain lives matter, and why do they get to decide? As Christians, we need to represent God's view—all lives are precious to Him.

> *The Lord is not slow in keeping his promise, as some understand slowness. Instead, he is patient with you, not wanting anyone to perish, but everyone to come to repentance* (2 Peter 2:9 NIV).

Not Statistically Different

The final nail in the coffin that there is something deceptive going on with the Covid narrative comes down to the numbers. Is Covid statistically different than diseases like pneumonia, flu, or a cold? Now comes the hard truth. In the 2017-2018 flu season, which is six months long, 2.56 million people died from pneumonia. So how long did it take COVID-19 to reach the same figures? Answer: close to 14 months.

• https://ourworldindata.org/pneumonia)

The world has proclaimed a pandemic even though there just isn't a statistical difference in overall mortality figures between 2020 and other years, a fact, that some are trying to cover up. However, if you go with the *New York Times* figure, 356,000 people died of the Coronavirus in 2020. Unfortunately, this number does not represent a statistical difference over other years. It doesn't even qualify as a spike or a pandemic.

Now for the next bit of deception. Remember, the flu and pneumonia go hand in hand. But Covid's narrative says this is so much worse than the flu, and it is. After all, the flu only kills up to 650,000 people globally in a typical year. The problem is that when you add in pneumonia, which is the 2.54 million we previously mentioned, then the whole equation flips. Essentially, between the two of them (see the numbers above), they can easily kill close to 3 million people worldwide. Compare this to the 1.8 million Covid deaths in 2020, and we can see the problem.

If these deaths rates are not unprecedented, then what is going on here? Why has no disease previously had 24/7 TV coverage, closed down the whole world, or caused us to alter our lives with masks and social distancing? Yet, these same procedures could apply to the flu or pneumonia. Even though other illnesses kill more people, we have seen a glaring double standard where "Covid lives" are concerned. These facts are why I am convinced that, at worst, there is a dark deception being played upon the world. At best, hysteria has gotten entirely out of control.

The Retracted Article

Note: The following article has been retracted since I initially wrote this section, but I do not believe that the numbers have changed enough for them justify this retraction. So, I have decided to still include it.

Johns Hopkins Took Down an Article Showing US Deaths in 2020 Were No Different Than Prior Years.

- https://www.thegatewaypundit.com/2020/11/johns-hop-kins-takes-article-showing-us-deaths-2020-no-different-prior-years-doesnt-fit-gonna-die-narrative/

If you still believe that some of the Covid narrative still holds water, well read what happens when the *John's Hopkins Newsletter* (November 22 by Yanni Gu) critically analyzed the effect of COVID-19 on US deaths using data from the CDC.

Surprisingly, the deaths of older people stayed the same before and after COVID-19. Since COVID-19 mainly affects the elderly, experts expected an increase in the percentage of deaths in older age groups... But, in fact, the percentages of deaths among all age groups remain relatively the same.

- https://web.archive.org/web/20201126223119/https://www.jhunewsletter.com/article/2020/11/a-closer-look-at-us-deaths-due-to-covid-19

We have been hearing for quite some time that the 2020 death rate in the US population has remained the same compared to the previous year. However, now that the death rate of the "at-risk" group has remained the same, we can definitively say that the Covid narrative is false. Is it real? Yes, but is it statistically different than the flu and pneumonia. No, it isn't. Now let that sink in. They have knowingly created a false crisis.

The 1% conundrum: How a simple but flawed math prediction by US Covid-19 experts caused the world to panic and order lockdowns.

- https://www.rt.com/op-ed/500000-covid19-math-mistake-panic/?fbclid=IwAR21OA3e1texwCed-hBS3hlYRFt5t3uMsaU8sY2WZY6iCQx4gKd_Qq22sqs

24/7 Coverage and Financial Incentives
The Big Surge in Coronavirus Deaths
Is a Media-Fed Myth

"The Florida Department of Health reported 156 new coronavirus-related deaths on Thursday, the most yet in a 24-hour period." Yet, Florida's health department reports only 68 deaths that day. The most deaths occurring in a single day in the state is 101, a drastic contradiction compared to what is reported each day.

- https://issuesinsights.com/2020/07/22/the-big-surge-in-coronavirus-deaths-is-a-media-fed-myth/amp/?__twitter_impression=true

Coronavirus Study Confirms, with the Exception of N.Y. and New Jersey, Overall Mortality Not Much Different Than a Bad Flu Season.

- https://www.eastonspectator.com/2020/07/15/exclusive-coronavirus-study-confirms-with-exception-of-new-york-and-new-jersey-overall-mortality-not-much-than-a-bad-flu-season/

This article says that these two states accounted for up to 40% of the total deaths in the country. Why? Because other states aren't sending COVID-19 patients back into nursing homes or putting as many people on respirators because of financial incentives. If there was one thing we learned from Italy, it was that the elderly population and smokers were at a higher risk of Covid. So, who was ultimately responsible for making the decisions that led to this unprecedented loss of life? Unfortunately, the same people who are blaming their political opponent were the ones who made all the decisions. I supported our past president when he decided that Covid is not a one size fits all solution. Each state, governor, city, and county should be allowed to make decisions based on their own situation. The problem is that some states made their decisions and then blamed it on the president.

- https://www.businessinsider.com/cuomo-nursing-home-deaths-coronavirus-covid-independent-investigation-death-2020-8

Prescribing respirators in mass were also part of the problem. Hospitals received $13,000 per person if they were admitted as a Covid case, and another $39,000 for every patient put on a ventilator. The problem is that only 12% of COVID-19 patients who were put on ventilators in New York's largest hospital system survived. Indeed, I have had a nurse tell me that she has only seen a couple of people come off respirators in her career.

- https://www.organiclifestylemagazine.com/cdc-admits-finacial-hospital-incentives-drove-up-covid-19-death-rates

- https://www.ozy.com/the-new-and-the-next/use-ventilators-or-not-the-big-question-covid-doctors-are-now-grappling-with/315946/

The Fate of a Nation

Sadly, politicians "never let a good crisis go to waste." It has not been a coincidence that all of the cities, counties, and states controlled by socialist leaders must be kept closed until after the election. When I mention these facts, I am usually met with the comment, "It is an election year." Election antics mean that America has become so divided that a group of people would rather destroy America than let the other party win fair and square. They are okay with lying, cheating, and stealing to get what they want. Unfortunately, they have accomplished their true goal, which is to divide and destroy America. Unfortunately, both parties are to blame.

Why do I say that division is the main goal? Because the old saying goes, "United we stand and divided we fall." As Christians, we hate to see America become divided, completely embroiled in bickering and embracing hate or violence. However, we still have the greatest freedoms of any people in world history. Of course, we do have a host of problems, but division and hate are not how we move forward.

Covid-19, like any other problem, must not be approached emotionally or irrationally. Unfortunately, division seems to be the explicit goal of the media. They are the ones who need to be defunded for putting out a false message aimed at dividing us. If anything is negative or would destroy and divide America, they will cover it 24/7. Unfortunately, the traditional media is not the only one that is involved.

Divide and Conquer

When it comes to seeing the bigger picture of what is happening, I recommend the movies, *The Social Dilemma* and *The Creepy Line*. Both of these films perfectly portray how the media and the internet are controlling and dividing America. Google and virtually most social media are tracking everything we do and collecting it in an artificial intelligence (AI).

This AI is manipulating and controlling us through the information that it allows us to see. They are especially intent on feeding us polarizing things. Determining what appears in our on-line searches means that we are being influenced without our knowledge, which is why "fake news" has taken a hold on America. Unfortunately, the conclusion of the *Social Dilemma* movie was that this manipulation would eventually cause a civil war in America.

Surprisingly, the writers of that film believed this to be an accident, but I don't think that for a minute. Foreign powers are also at play. The sudden influx of worldwide input on social media regarding our elections has also been well documented. By now, the situation should seem obvious; someone or something is trying to destroy America. Who would like to eliminate or divide America? Some apparent possibilities are China, Russia, or the New World Order.

With China being the new #1 superpower, current political voices say America must join a united Europe to balance that kind of power. Thus far, it would seem that Covid-19 is playing its part by bringing about division and financial ruin wherever it goes in the free world. So, how do we fight this deception? Answer: by offering the perspective that all lives matter and are precious to God. People are dying every day, but people don't know why or how they can help.

We have the opportunity to still save lives and to show God's love. We cannot save everyone, but we can make strategic decisions about how to impact the most lives we can. Only focusing on Covid-19 lives has caused us to lose sight of the bigger picture to the point of destroying everything. We need to break this deception by representing those who have no voice. For most of us, all lives still matter, and this is how we can build bridges to better understanding. In the process, we can also destroy a potent deception.

A Cure Worse Than the Disease

Early in the pandemic, thousands of doctors wrote a letter to Trump to end the lockdowns. The reason is that 150,000 people are diagnosed with cancer each month. Not getting that timely diagnosis will lead to their death. I recently had to go on blood pressure meds because I could not go to the gym during Covid shutdowns. Even skipping routine dental care can lead to increased strokes and heart attacks.

Furthermore, virtually no one is talking about depression, alcohol abuse, or drug abuse as some of the adverse effects of Covid shutdowns. Some people didn't even go outside. Being a shut-in deprives people of exercise and vitamins, which can help boost their immunity. While this is the tip of the iceberg, it becomes easier to see that we may be killing more people in one month than Covid has killed in closer to a year.

- https://kmph.com/news/nation-world/letter-from-doctors-calls-on-president-trump-to-end-lockdown

If you still think you have been hearing the truth about what other doctors besides Dr. Anthony Fauci believe, then ask yourself why you haven't heard of the "Great Barrington Declaration." This document was initially authored by doctors and epidemiologists from Oxford, Harvard, and Princeton. Since its inception, more than 55,000 medical doctors and health scientists from around the world have signed this declaration. The petition is to end lockdowns because they are causing "irreparable damage."

They have specifically listed some of their reasoning to include: "worsening cardiovascular disease outcomes, fewer cancer screenings, and deteriorating mental health." Not following these guidelines will lead to excess mortality in years to come. They also went on to say that "Keeping students out of school is a grave injustice," because "We know that vulnerability to death from COVID-19 is more than a thousand-fold higher in the old than the young."

In fact, for "children, COVID-19 is less dangerous than many other harms, including influenza." I'm still speechless that no one knows this. They are not the only ones trying to get kids back to school. The CDC director said that all kids should have been back in school by September 2020 and that "School is the safest place for children to be." Unfortunately, our children are being held hostage with a false fear, while they are suffering irreparable damage to their education.

- https://nypost.com/2021/04/07/schools-should-be-fully-in-person-by-september-cdc-director/

- https://www.msn.com/en-us/news/us/school-is-safest-place-for-children-to-be-cdc-director-says/ar-BB1bbjnq

What the Barrington panel of experts did recommend is an approach they call "Focused Protection." Essentially, they believe that all populations will reach herd immunity through natural processes. Consequently, they recommend allowing those at minimal risk of death to live their lives normally to develop immunity to the virus as part of natural infection. In addition, permitting those who are not at risk to catch Covid will cause it to pass through our population quicker, thereby lowering the risks to everyone.

But, of course, we need to take some significant protective measures for those with a high risk of dying from COVID-19. So, the question is, "Why is it that these doctors' opinions don't matter?" What am I trying to say? I am saying that the cure they have administered is worse than the disease. The Covid shutdowns alone have caused "a six-fold increase in people living in famine-like conditions since the pandemic began in 2020." This blatant ignorance of the bigger picture is why 55,000 doctors disagree with Fauci.

- https://greekreporter.com/2021/07/10/hunger-crises-caused-more-deaths-coronavirus-2020/

But keeping people from seeing their doctors is not the only way that we are killing more than we save. Even the UN is not recommending more shutdowns for Covid because millions more will starve this year than usual. Winning the battle against the Covid narrative is causing us to lose the war against world hunger. Currently, hunger is killing 4-5 times as many people as Covid-19. Unfortunately, we are not allowed to talk about this.

- https://news.un.org/en/story/2020/09/1072712

- https://www.reuters.com/article/us-health-coronavirus-children-un/u-n-warns-economic-downturn-could-kill-hundreds-of-thousands-of-children-in-2020-idUSKBN21Y2X7

Now think about this verse. "My people perish for lack of knowledge" (Hosea 4:6). Lack of correct information is what is wrong with the COVID-19 narrative. The truth is that no one in America has heard there are other possibilities of how to respond to Covid. For example, Sweden and Norway didn't shut down the way we did and had fewer deaths and less economic impact. But, of course, Sweden did not take all of the business away from the hospitals or give a lot more money for a Covid diagnosis.

In America, everyone was too quick to take a stimulus as if there is such a thing as free money. Once the government announced the stimulus, nine out of my thirteen therapists decided to stay home because they could make more money doing nothing. In this regard, the stimulus has bought most of us off and kept us silent. Borrowing from our children has merely delayed the financial consequences of shutting down. But like all debt, it will be a bitter pill to swallow in the future.

Indeed, financial destruction is the goal of how we are handling Covid. People are losing their jobs, businesses, houses, and cars even though they have no risk of dying from Covid. They are being forced into bankruptcy because they aren't allowed to work. But the facts remain that people under 40 have virtually a zero percent risk of dying from COVID-19. In contrast, people over 65 comprise 80% of Covid deaths.

- https://www.cdc.gov/coronavirus/2019-ncov/need-extra-precautions/older-adults.html

This one size fits all mentality is not the way doctors usually practice medicine. Imagine if we had to treat all patients like we did the elderly. Making a differential diagnosis is what keeps a doctor from being charged with malpractice. Besides age, the other significant risk factors are lung disease, obesity, auto-immune disorders, diabetes, and heart disease. Age considering, if you don't have one of these risk factors, you have almost no chance of dying from Covid. So, why would the media be making 100% of us afraid when very few of us will die? We must be over 85 to have a risk rate of more than 1%.

Why would we destroy America or borrow money from our children over something with such a slight risk for most of us? Why is there so much disinformation about Covid-19? Why is the media lying to us, and why are both political parties capitulating with it? Why are we being blinded by both science and the facts? Why are most people utterly wrong about what their risk level really is? This deception is precisely what we will address moving forward because people are needlessly living in fear.

Not only are lies the source of this conspiracy, but this is correlated with what the Bible means when it says, "They have traded the truth for a lie" (Romans 1:25). Disinformation has always been one of the fundamental techniques used by everyone from communists to Satanists, to destroy a country. The film called *Disinformation: The Secret Strategy to Destroy the West* brought out this strategy to destroy America back in the late 80s. Russia's plan was to start all kinds of non-profit world groups aimed at putting out false information to undermine freedom, faith, and capitalism.

We Are at War

Currently, General H.R. McMaster, the former National

Security Advisor, has written a book called *Battlegrounds*, in which he affirms that the US is actually at war. Not a direct conflict, but an information war through social media, operatives, and the internet. His final message is that America needs to wake up, catch up, and stop being so selfish because there is a war for the truth. Unfortunately, this false information is also destroying the world and the church.

Indeed, most Christians are unaware of the already heavy persecution of Christians. Some of this is because they have been taught that it is impossible for Christians to see the tribulation, but recent events are starting to rule this possibility out. Even though there is going to be an escape (Luke 21:36) or rapture (1 Thessalonians 4:17) because Christians were not appointed to wrath (1 Thessalonians 5:9), it is time to realize that all Christians are likely to experience some tribulation before this is over.

We also have to face the fact that a growing population of Americans hate their own country. These dissenters could quickly go somewhere else in the world where their ideal government already exists. The reason they don't is that none of these countries hold a candle to ours. Still, Americans act like we have no enemies when we are the last of our kind. Unfortunately, no one in the free world has dared to question the Covid narrative, check the facts, or ponder the long-term consequences.

Yet, with all of the deception, most of us still don't believe it. Just watch what happens when masks become optional. Still, the financial damage has been done, and this alone can destroy us. Most Christians recognize that America isn't specifically listed in the Bible's end times, so what happens to us? Without America, the world would be fully communist right now because no other country could stop Russia or China from invading them. Communism and technology are why the world as we know it is at risk, and why Covid is a distraction from the true agenda.

How can you know that Covid-19 is a deception? First, the

powers behind this conspiracy have engineered inflation of the Covid deaths by changing the guidelines of how death certificates are written and by offering more money for a Covid diagnosis. The second is that we are not being told about any other deaths except Covid-19. The third is that the Covid death toll is not statistically different than other years of pneumonia/flu. The last is that 94% of the Covid deaths did not die of Covid. According to the old rules, they would have died of underlying conditions because the underlying condition was always listed as the cause of death, not an immediate or active condition.

We will cover this rule change shortly. But the most significant proof there is a deception is how the average person has overestimated their risk of dying from Covid to a shocking extent. The following article shows how we are being blinded to the facts concerning our actual level of risk. Essentially, the following study found that this deception is worse for Democrats, partisanship (those who are biased for their cause, such as their dislike for the current president), and for people on social media.

- On average, Americans believe that people aged 55 and older account for just over half of total COVID-19 deaths; the actual figure is 92%.

- Americans believe that people aged 44 and younger account for about 30% of total deaths; the actual figure is 2.7%.

- Americans overestimate the risk of death from COVID-19 for people aged 24 and younger by a factor of 50. They also think the chance for people aged 65 and older is half of what it actually is (40% vs. 80%).

They Blinded Us from Science:
How Americans misperceive the risks of death from COVID-19 to a shocking extent.

- https://www.franklintempletonnordic.com/investor/article-?contentPath=html%2Fftthinks%2Fcommon%2Fcio-views%2Fon-my-mind-they-blinded-us-from-science.html&fbclid=IwAR2ZI8qtH7Y7jBls0LvO3vqVpARJ-Yb0dUdBIz-9Y-REFQlZBH6ayCgFR3o

The Real Reason for Covid?

If COVID-19 is not worse than the flu/pneumonia was in the 2017-2018 flu season, then what is going on here? If we really could save more lives by opening up and encouraging people to see their doctors, then why are we closed down? If 94% of people who died of Covid didn't die of *only* Covid, why isn't the main dialog about the factors that 94% of people had versus the 6%? The answer to all of these questions is that Covid is not about saving lives; it is about creating fear and chaos.

The question then becomes, why chaos? Because we get the order out of chaos. The Latin saying, *Ordo ab Chao* is one of the oldest ideas for manipulating a society. "Order out of Chaos" is a motto directly attributed to the Masons, who also happen to call themselves an order. Specifically, the title is the Thirty-third Degree of the Supreme Council of the Scottish Rite of Free Masons. Whether it is the Masons, the Bilderberg's, the Illuminati, or the New World Order, most people have to accept that there is a group of people in the world that believe humanity is going to destroy itself if they don't intervene.

Of course, there is too much global warming, weapons of mass destruction, and tampering with mother earth, so they feel we must all be controlled. These are the kinds of things that become possible when 62 people in the world (the same ones that Bernie

Sanders referred to in the 2016 election) have more money than 3.6 million of us. What Bernie forgot to mention is that he works for those people. People who are like this only fear one thing: freedom and means. That is why destroying America is precisely the goal of socialism and communism.

The Hegelian Dialectic is another form of manipulation that is used to accomplish a nefarious agenda. In its simplest form, the Hegelian Dialectic says, "If you want to do something, create a problem where the natural solution to the problem is what you wanted to do in the first place." If we are looking for signs of the return of Jesus, then the rise of a one-world government should be high on our list. The Bible calls this government the "Beast" in Revelation and the "Divided Kingdom" in Daniel.

In each case, this government has ten horns or ten toes. Curiously, the United Nations has divided the world into ten regions. This New World Order appears to be developing around ancient Rome in the form of the EU. This is important because, according to Daniel, the last kingdom would have a connection to the old Roman Empire. However, what should be obvious is that the biggest obstacle to a one-world government is the United States of America.

Looking at this final government, one would have to admit that it is very similar to communism, except for a deep state religion. But, again, the only thing resisting this one world government is the US. No other countries can defend themselves against Russia or China. Sadly, millennials and now generation Z are open to socialism and communism. Yet, the reality is that communism is the greatest evil the world has ever seen because it has killed over 100 million people. So, why do we not hear of this evil? Why do we hear more about the Holocaust, American slavery, or how we wiped out the Native Americans?

While America has tried to spread freedom and capitalism around the world, it hasn't worked. We really are one of a kind. Yet, the biggest delusion of most Americans is that we do not know we are not number one in the world anymore. Who did we borrow money from when we needed money? It was China. Beijing has 21 times as many skyscrapers as New York City. How much longer are the most entitled people in the world going to continue to say, "In the richest country in the world, why can't we afford to do _____?" Yet, no country can spend more than it makes. No country can continue to have massive trade deficits forever. No, one day, the Prodigal child will run out of their fathers' or their children's money.

The one great hope I have for America is that it will remember its spiritual heritage when it all falls apart. Unfortunately, the idea of nationalism or loving our country is now an insult when it used to be a cry to arms. Yet, the entire world is dependent upon America for its freedoms. Just think about how prosperous America would be if we didn't have to defend ourselves. Think about what the world would be like if China played by the rules and didn't steal everyone's technology.

Glenn Beck Warns of Socialism/Communism and How They Did It in Venezuela.

- https://podcasts.apple.com/us/podcast/theblaze-radio-specials/id999341784?i=1000437102474

A Recipe for Destruction

There are two main ways to destroy any country without ever going to war. The first is to divide the people within it, and the second is to destroy it financially. Unfortunately, division and financial implosion are both happening as we speak. Indeed, we have never seen a more intense and violent divide among Americans. They are dividing us based on races, vaccines, and the "haves versus the have nots." Even the police have become a target. Not only is our society being divided, but our national debt is out of control, and the shutdowns are sealing our fate.

But no one cares about that or the fact that we have open borders. Essentially, Covid is the only issue that is allowed to matter even though the fox is in the hen house. Most people do not know our national debt is held by the Federal Reserve, which is privately owned. Essentially, we don't own our country anymore. Unfortunately, these are the same people that own the IMF or International Monetary Fund. The great uncertainty is who are these people, and what do they want in return.

Chaos and Control

It is apparent we are in chaos, and now our government requires a new level of control. In one year, the chaos has accumulated $15.1 trillion in governmental losses, shut down our businesses, forced us to wear masks, closed the churches, and distanced us from each other. But now they want us penetrated and marked. They want access to our bodies so that they can monitor and control what we can buy or sell, how much currency we have, and even our genetic content. You heard that last one right.

When I tell people that this supposed vaccine is genetic therapy and that it overwrites their God-given mRNA codes, they usually do not react because they are unfamiliar with the genetic narratives of the Bible. However, we will explore them thoroughly along with what the Bible says about the Mark of the Beast (MOB). Essentially, I have been saying for the past twelve years that the MOB is not just going to be nanotechnology. The MOB is going to have genetic markers.

I first heard this idea after listening to a Bible prophecy series by Tom Horn. The scariest thing that I would find out about changing our DNA is that it would change the image we were created in. But what I obviously knew is that God wrote our genetic codes, and then He called them good. Changing what God wrote can be called blasphemy. Logically, changing our DNA could also change who our father is, and who we are related to.

25

God Hasn't Changed

While the world is changing dramatically, what is ultimately important to God never does. During these trying times, we cannot lose our focus on all lives because this is part of what distinguishes us. While we cannot stop Covid, we can do our best to save the lives we can. The problem is we aren't doing that. In fact, we are making everything worse. Essentially, we are throwing the baby out with the bathwater because it is perspective that we have lost. While the media won't cover much except Covid, we need to take up the cause of freedom and to represent those who can't represent themselves. We could easily get rid of malaria, waterborne illnesses, and world hunger.

We could have saved 36 times as many lives for 1.8% of what we spent on Covid. Fighting for "all lives" will also destroy the most grievous accusations against us, which is that we are a hate group. Doing what only love can do is what will bring back the truth. Truth is what works, and lies are what lead to bad decisions and even worse consequences. Yet, there is nothing more hateful than the idea of political correctness. We must return to talking about love, freedom, respect, and mercy regardless of someone's view because there is one thing that love would never do. Love would never take away our ability to choose, and that includes between love or hate.

"I will permit no man to narrow and degrade my soul by making me hate him." —*Booker T. Washington*

"You can't hold a man down without staying down with him." —*Booker T. Washington*

Privilege and Providence
Rather Die from COVID-19 Than Loneliness:
Seniors Protest against Coronavirus Lockdowns

- https://www.washingtonexaminer.com/news/rather-die-from-covid-than-loneliness-seniors-protest-against-coronavirus-lockdowns-outside-nursing-home

Many people have died all alone this past year. All of this has been mandated without asking them or their family what they thought. Meanwhile, marches for social justice took place with no questions asked. They are allowed to violently protest what they see as wrong with our society. But the truth is that everyone should have a choice about how they die, and that is another part of what Covid is taking away. Unfortunately, I have had many a conversation about the deep hurt and frustration of not being able to see a loved one that is dying.

The value of the family is one of the privileges that America has lost sight of. Yet, the number one predictor of success in life is being born into a family where we are loved, guided, and disciplined. The Asian slaves arrived in America somewhat around the time of other slaves. But they were the last to get the right to vote or own property. Many of them were in concentration camps during WWII, but today, they make more money than any other race. The reason is because of family. Asians have the most intact families in America, with the fewest divorces and the fewest abortions. The power of the family holds up even in a secular world.

For example, children of black nuclear families have only a 12% chance of living below poverty, versus 45% for a black single mom and 36% for a single black dad. The fatherless youth represent 90% of the homeless and runaways; 85% of those with behavioral problems; 80% of rapists with anger problems; 71% of high school dropouts; 85% of youths in prison; 71% of pregnant teenagers; 90% of repeat arsonists.

- https://www.aei.org/articles/the-power-of-the-two-parent-home-is-not-a-myth/

- https://thefatherlessgeneration.wordpress.com

These are the facts that matter, which is why the first thing God did when He made humanity was to form a family. Promoting the family is also one of the things that most people are open to discuss. Of course, God is all about family. However, we have an epidemic of un-parented prodigal children that need to come home. The problem is they haven't even heard about their heavenly Father.

While I believe capitalism is an excellent economic system, it has inextricably led us to worship money, power, fame, and career. Materialism is destroying and distracting America because our families are the very fabric or foundation of our society. Still, we cannot recover the brotherhood of man until we restore the Fatherhood of God. The good news is that God is still waiting for all of His children to come home with open arms. God's message that all lives are precious is powerful, but the missing ingredient is when Christians humble themselves and pray.

Unfortunately, God's message is counter to the media or political narrative because they are full of deception, division, and hate. Consequently, we must become genuinely counter-cultural like Jesus. Of course, we still need to figure out how to engage our society with respect to Covid, politics, vaccinations, and privilege. We also need to be prepared because people will walk away from us.

The chaos around us is how the New World Order wants to control us. Yet, something sinister is coming that will change everything concerning the saving of our souls. The Mark of the Beast (MOB) is a barrier that the Gospel cannot overcome. Could the Covid narrative have anything to do with this "great deception" that the Bible says is coming?

The Greater Deception

The Covid deception has divided us, destroyed us financially, and caused us to go cashless and touchless. Still, there is an even bigger deception afoot. What do I mean? Something akin to the mark of the beast may very well be here, and they will make it mandatory. A mandatory vaccine implies that we no longer have rights to our bodies. If this is the case, then it doesn't matter whether this vaccine is the mark of the beast or not. We will be allowing them to pass a law that will force us to be marked later.

Time is running out. If we are going to save our freedoms, then we will not believe what is on TV. We may have to be prepared to resist because something is coming that we cannot go along with. Not facing this beast will only make matters worse because the beast is growing in power every day. Yet, most churches are failing to address the situation because it is a public relations nightmare. Political correctness is keeping religion out of politics, but that isn't biblical. Jesus was killed for political reasons.

The other question is, what can the church confront in our society without losing church members. Unfortunately, this kind of thinking is not going to work anymore. Either people will believe their Bibles, or they will allow their government access to their bodies. The fact that RNA is part of this new vaccine is not a coincidence. Yet, the sad truth is that some vaccines are already mandatory, and almost everybody gets them.

The shocking fact that the church has not yet arrived at is that taking the mark of the beast will destroy our ability to save anyone. Essentially, salvation may come down to our ability to convince someone that they should not capitulate with the law or what they see on TV. Without a firm belief in Bible prophecy, the church cannot make this transition. We cannot be saved if we take the mark of the beast (Revelation 14:9-11). Think this truth isn't being censored? I found it difficult to find this verse on google, so I had to use duckduckgo.

2

The Mark of Deception

There is an elephant in the room, and the church refuses to talk about it. However, if we don't address it soon, the church will become irrelevant because we are not talking about the real issues that are keeping people up at night. Of course, most of us would like to go back to pretending that things will return to normal, but this is unlikely to be the case. Soon, a hard decision is coming—a fork in the road that may forever change our fate and our destiny. This decision is about whether to take a vaccine or not.

Unfortunately, our entire society has been held hostage for over a year due to the COVID-19 narrative. Now we are being told that things cannot go back to normal unless we are all vaccinated. Yet, the Covid narrative and agenda are false with respect to being different than the flu/pneumonia. This deception is precisely what we covered in our last chapter. Not only are the COVID-19 deaths not statistically different than other flu/pneumonia seasons, but we will cover how the PCR test for Covid is inaccurate.

If health insurance companies gave significantly more money for a COVID-19 diagnosis, and hospitals retooled their entire billing department to take advantage of COVID-19 money, then what do you think that did to the overall COVID-19 numbers? We already covered how even the CDC director admitted that the COVID-19 numbers increased because of financial incentives. But now, let's cover how they legally changed how they did death certificates.

The CDC Changed the Rules

Dr. Andrew Kaufman explains how the CDC, after close to 50 years, suddenly changed the rules about how a death certificate was filled out. This happened as soon as Covid was declared a public health crisis. The CDC then issued a guidance change. Specifically, health care workers were told that if there was a suspicion of Covid, then they should put Covid as the cause of death. Astonishing? Suspicion alone has never been used to determine a cause of death.

The purpose of this report is to provide guidance to death certifiers on proper cause-of-death certification for cases where confirmed or suspected COVID–19 infection resulted in death.

• https://www.cdc.gov/nchs/data/nvss/vsrg/vsrg03-508.pdf

The other major change involved giving an "immediate" cause of death preference over an "underlying" condition. This change alone has allowed them to perpetuate the idea that normal, healthy people are dying of Covid, but this is not the case. Normally, if someone has cancer as the underlying condition, you do not say they died of an infection, the flu, or cold because normal people do not die of these things. The same is true of Covid.

• Dr. Andrew Kaufman interview: https://www.bitchute.com/video/FGCjXTR7kUO2/

Another strange change was that they prevented autopsies of Covid deaths. Now, just in case you were wondering, they did still keep track of comorbidities and underlying conditions. This is why we can still somewhat see what would have happened if they hadn't changed anything. This old analysis versus the new analysis is why the CDC later admitted that 94% of the people that died of Covid had other comorbidities, which means that only 6% of the deaths were due to only Covid and no other conditions.

The fact remains that if they hadn't changed the rules about how to fill out a death certificate, then they would have never been able to produce sufficient deaths to declare a pandemic to the public. Without these changes, we could be looking at something around 22,500 total Covid only deaths, which is 6% of 375,000—not something that would have changed the world. These guidance changes, along with the significant financial incentives offered for a Covid diagnosis, can completely explain the high numbers of deaths attributed to Covid. Any way we look at it, there is no way they can claim 100% of their numbers.

The Covid Narrative Is False

All of this has led me to the inextricable conclusion that the COVID-19 narrative is completely false (to the point of being manufactured) with respect to being statistically different than the flu/pneumonia. Normal healthy individuals who are under 65 do not have any significant risk of dying from Covid. If this is true, then who is in on it? If Joe Biden, Donald Trump, every conservative, every liberal, every TV station, every news source, every internet company, every health insurance company, every hospital, and every internet search engine are complicit with the Covid narrative, then what are we up against? Are you starting to get the picture?

Still, it is the COVID-19 narrative that overturned an incumbent president, forcibly closed our churches and schools, allowed for mail-in ballots, added trillions to the national debt, divided our people, and destroyed the greatest economy the USA had ever had. Most importantly, COVID-19 damaged the church and the faith of those who were attending. Even now, COVID-19 is dividing the church, and people are questioning their faith more than ever before. Furthermore, the COVID-19 narrative has also produced regulations that have destroyed many of our religious freedoms in this country.

In unprecedented fashion, churches and even home Bible studies were shut down, and citizens were fined if they attended. Churches in California had to declare themselves temporary "strip clubs" because strip clubs were open, and they were not. Yet, God did not leave us without a warning to be on guard for a massive deception that is to be played out upon us all in the end times. The Bible says that a delusion is coming that is so powerful and so persuasive that if it were possible, it would deceive the very elect of God's children.

The coming of the lawless one will be accompanied by the working of Satan, with every kind of power, sign, and false wonder, and with every wicked deception directed against those who are perishing, because they refused the love of the truth that would have saved them. For this reason, God will send them a powerful delusion so that they believe the lie, so that judgment may come upon all who have disbelieved the truth and delighted in wickedness (2 Thessalonians 2:9-11, but read the whole chapter).

For false messiahs and false prophets will appear and perform great signs and wonders to deceive, if possible, even the elect (Matthew 24:24 BSB).

We have all been put in a difficult place because of the political pressure associated with defying the Covid agendas. Unfortunately, some people are true believers in the Covid narrative. Consequently, we can't even talk to some people about Covid without triggering an overreaction. Essentially, the disinformation warfare surrounding the Covid narrative has created a wall of fear that keeps us from exposing the truth, which is why I am praying for our ministers to begin to speak the truth in love.

Of course, large churches are especially at risk because people are still worried about gathering in big groups and being politically correct. We must remember that God chose the time in which we were born. This is the sense of destiny we can have if we are "in Christ" and are aware of God's prophetic clock. More importantly, we are called to fight for the minds and hearts of God's children, and this means we can't remain neutral any longer. The wolf is leading the sheep astray as we speak.

The Real Risk of Dying from Covid

These numbers are calculated based on the number of deaths due to COVID-19 (568,053 deaths) divided by the United States population (332,769,579). Indeed, the overall chance of dying from Covid is 0.17% over the past 18 months. Additionally, here are the sources for the chart below that included age specific risks.

- https://www.statista.com/statistics/1191568/reported-deaths-from-covid-by-age-us/

- https://www.statista.com/statistics/241488/population-of-the-us-by-sex-and-age/

Age	Total Deaths	Population (million)	Chance of Dying
0-17	287	73.086	.000393 %
18-29	2163	53.554	.0040 %
30-39	6299	44.16	.014 %
40-49	16,987	40.32	.042 %
50-64	87,915	62.92	.139 %
65-74	125,939	31.49	.39 %
75-84	156,777	15.97	.98 %
85+	171,686	6.61	2.59 %**

Additionally, these numbers are inflated due to the guidance changes the CDC made to death certificates, as well as the financial incentives offered to health care providers by insurance companies.

**Remember, if you have no underlying conditions, your chance of dying from Covid is significantly lower than the above chart.

Lifetime Odds of Death for Selected Causes
United States, 2019

Heart disease	1 in 6	16.6%
Suicide	1 in 88	1.13%
Drug Overdose	1 in 92	1.08%
Fall	1 in 106	.94%
Pedestrian Incident	1 in 543	.18%
Motorcycle	1 in 899	.11%
Drowning	1 in 1,128	.088%
Bicyclist	1 in 3,825	.026%
Dog Attach	1 in 86,781	.0011%
Lightning	1 in 138,849	.00072

- https://injuryfacts.nsc.org/all-injuries/preventable-death-overview/odds-of-dying/

Medical Malpractice

We could sum up a lot of what is wrong with the Covid narrative based upon these risk levels. Essentially, everything in medicine is based upon making what is called a *differential diagnosis*. Without a differential diagnosis, everyone would be treated the same if they had the same symptoms or positive test. For example, if someone comes into a doctor's office and tests positive for cancer, it could mean almost anything. The follow-up questions are where is the cancer, what kind of cancer is it, what stage is it in, and what is the health and age of the person?

Without this differential diagnosis, every cancer patient would get surgery, chemo, and radiation, which could end up killing more people. This is exactly what is happening with the Covid narrative. We have to treat everyone as if they are over 85, but even then, only 2.5% succumb to Covid. We also have to remember that most of the symptoms people get from Covid are similar to a cold, flu, or pneumonia, which are not fun, but people get them every day. The two differential factors that are being ignored are age and underlying conditions (comorbidities). Even one underlying condition is not always a huge problem, but plus two dramatically increases the risk.

The problem is that there is only one treatment being mandated for everyone, and even they don't all need it. But our government is okay with the idea of forcing someone to treat something that will not kill or harm them. Not only is it medical malpractice, but it is also a crime against humanity. The crime against humanity comes into full play because said treatment is of an experimental nature. In other words, people are losing their jobs, businesses, rights, and sanity because 0.17% of us died over 18 months of Covid. My question is, where are the doctors and why can't they see that this is breaking the Hippocratic Oath? If we just compare apples to apples, it is easy to see why everything we are doing to solve Covid doesn't make sense.

The Implications

- Can you imagine the media covering every pedestrian, bicycle, and motorcycle accident for a year and a half, and the kind of fear they would have generated around those activities?

- Essentially, dogs, swimming pools, walking, or riding a bike or motorcycle would be illegal.

- Can you imagine keeping kids out of school for over a year because of a fear of lightning? So, what is the real reason they didn't go to school?

- Bottom line, all of these items except the bottom 3 are more dangerous than Covid if you are under 50.

- If motorcycles, bikes, and dogs are still legal, why is it illegal to work, go without a mask, or refuse to take an emergency use only vaccine when natural immunity works just fine?

- If we are under 85, we are more likely to die of suicide or a drug overdose than Covid.

- Can you imagine if every new station or TV show had to be specifically targeted to fight depression, drugs, and suicide?

The COVID-19 Agenda

Like any deception, the COVID-19 agenda has predictably followed the rules of performing magic. A magician always distracts us with his one hand when he is doing all the real work of deception with the other hand. Understanding who is in on the Covid deception will tell us Satan's real agenda. Essentially, we have to stop being fooled by this good cop and bad cop routine in American politics. We must also recognize that our enemies have been trying to destroy us and our freedoms since the founding of our country.

America is significant because we are the biggest obstacle to a one-world government that the Bible says is coming. The financial part of this agenda was laid out by the World Economic Forum in their plan for the Great Reset. Letting no crisis go to waste speeds up their plan to reset the world economies to their liking. Destroying us financially would dethrone America and destroy our influence.

- https://www.weforum.org/agenda/2021/01/davos-agenda-2021-society-and-the-future-of-work-skills-gap-jobs-of-tomorrow-diversity-inclusion-worker-well-being/

Disinformation and Desensitization

Since the advent of COVID-19, look at how people have been dehumanized and desensitized just by becoming masked entities instead of people full of contagious smiles. The Covid narrative purposely tries to destroy our social network and familial ties to isolate us, leaving us with nothing but our TV set. With Covid, we cannot afford to get too close to anyone. Suddenly, everyone needs their personal space, and people will let you know it. We are told to have a virtual Thanksgiving and give virtual high-fives. We cannot dare to meet in person or go on vacation. This is all intentional. Every day is an all-out assault on our sensibilities and our reason.

The practice of disinformation, or the art of telling lies, remains the number one way to disrupt and control entire societies. Remember, Satan is the father of lies. Now, these lies are being played out on us right here at home. For example, many TV stations have a Covid tracking window on their main screen all of the time. We are simply not allowed to stop thinking about Covid 24/7, even though 80% of the people are asymptomatic. Additionally, we are still forced to wear masks, even though they do not work, as we will see.

Mask Mandates

Even masks are being used to divide us as we speak. Why? Because people trust what is on TV. For some, the panic is palpable. People are living with so much fear that they feel like they must do something even though it does not work. When I tell someone that the type of mask they are wearing is only able to filter something 800 times bigger than this virus, they usually just clutch it more tightly or they just get mad (see next reference).

Shockingly, there are no face masks on the market that can filter something this small. So then, in mind-numbing dribble, Dr. Fauci comes out and tells us to wear three of them, only to change his mind within a week. To date, there is no peer-reviewed research that supports the effectiveness of wearing a mask to prevent COVID-19, and yet, we are forced to capitulate with the lies. How rude or ignorant we are made to feel if we dare question such things.

But questioning the mask mandate reveals the opposite. After 41 different studies, masks are shown not to be effective in reducing the contamination of influenza. The following is a quote from the *British Medical Journal.*

A systematic review published on 6 April 2020 examined whether wearing a face mask or other barrier (goggles, shield, veil) prevents transmission of respiratory illness such as coronavirus, rhinovirus, tuberculosis, or influenza. It identified **31 eligible studies,** including 12 randomized controlled trials. The authors found that overall, mask-wearing both in general and by infected members within households seemed to **produce small but statistically non-significant reductions in infection rates.** The authors concluded that **"The evidence is not sufficiently strong to support the widespread use of facemasks as a protective measure against covid-19."**

• https://www.bmj.com/content/369/bmj.m1435

In the same article, they also reviewed non-pharmaceutical measures for the prevention of influenza. They identified ten randomized controlled trials published between 1946 and 2018 that tested the efficacy of face masks for preventing laboratory-confirmed influenza. This "pooled meta-analysis found no significant reduction in influenza transmission." While the article was still recommending caution, the authors of the research they were referencing concluded: **"randomized controlled trials of [face masks] did not support a substantial effect on the transmission of laboratory-confirmed influenza."**

It is research like this that was used by the Canadian nurses' union to win their dispute with the hospitals that were requiring them to both vaccinate and wear masks. Mask research was also why virtually no one was recommending the use of masks when Covid first started. The precedent had already been set. Masks don't work, and neither do lockdowns, but they do have a psychological effect. For example, at one point, California had the strictest lockdowns and the most active cases of Covid by far.

- https://www.canadianlawyermag.com/practice-areas/adr/nurses-win-dispute-over-vaccinate-or-mask-policy/269926

- https://fee.org/articles/california-has-the-strictest-lockdown-in-the-us-and-the-most-active-covid-cases-by-far

No Consistency

When I see someone wearing a mask out in the middle of nowhere or by themselves in a car, I cannot help but chuckle to myself because they are the "true believers." On the other hand, if you are the only person in the Wawa station not wearing a mask, you will get more dirty looks in five minutes than you will usually get all year. Unfortunately, trying to figure out how, when, and where to wear a mask is confusing because it changes everywhere we go. For example, the sign on the gym says, "No Mask, No Entry, No Exceptions." Yet, once you scan your key card, everyone takes their mask off and works out like normal.

This double standard is the same for restaurants that require you to wear a mask for the short walk to the table. My family enjoyed water parks because they didn't require masks once you cross a certain line, where magically everything goes back to normal. Yet, the same dry amusement park next door was like walking around with the mask Nazi's nipping at your heels. All of this has fostered a Gestapo mentality all over something that is a complete façade. The following are some good articles about masks.

New CDC Study Finds Majority of Those Infected with COVID-19 "Always" Wore Masks

People diagnosed with COVID-19 were asked about their use

of masks 14 days before catching Covid. Here are their answers: Never – 3.9%, Rarely – 3.9%, Always – 70.6%

- https://californiaglobe.com/section-2/new-cdc-study-finds-majority-of-those-infected-with-covid-19-always-wore-masks/

A Month Since Texas Governor Lifted Mask Mandate and Covid Cases Continue to Fall

- https://www.dailywire.com/news/its-been-nearly-a-month-since-texas-governor-lifted-mask-mandate-and-covid-cases-continue-to-fall?fbclid=IwAR0YU6-qV4ujU6 0viVMjhdk9eDrj-BOin_yuT1M32Au8G9Tij9Eqv Wf6Ob0

Top Scientists Join DeSantis to Slam Masks, Mandates, and Covid Tyranny

- https://thenewamerican.com/top-scientists-join-desantis-to-slam-masks-mandates-and-covid-tyranny/

- Disposable Blue Face Masks Found to Contain Toxic, Asbestos-Like Substance That Destroys Lungs

- https://www.theubernews.com/bombshell/

NIH Stanford Study Proves Face Masks Worthless Against Covid

- https://principia-scientific.com/nih-stanford-study-proves-face-masks-worthless-against-covid/

Size Matters

Here are the findings of the American Association of Physicians and Surgeons. COVID-19 is as politically charged as it is infectious. Early in the COVID-19 pandemic, the WHO, the CDC, and Dr. Anthony Fauci discouraged wearing masks. Later, they recommend wearing cloth masks and social distancing. These recommendations were published without a single scientific paper to support the use of cloth masks. Here are their conclusions:

- The preponderance of scientific evidence supports that aerosols play a critical role in the transmission of COVID-19. If anything gets through, you will become infected. Therefore, a mask must provide a high level of filtration and fit to be highly effective.

- A COVID-19 (SARS-CoV-2) particle is 0.125 micrometers/microns (m); influenza virus size is 0.08 – 0.12 m; a human hair is about 150 m, but cloth masks aren't effective at blocking particles smaller than 100 m.

- Essentially, Covid is 800 times too small, and virtually all masks are loose-fitting devices.

- Even a properly fitted N95 will only block particles down to 0.3 m, (3-4 times too big)

- Consequently, there is virtually no mask on the market that can filter COVID-19.

- Source: https://aapsonline.org/mask-facts/

A cluster-randomized trial of cloth masks compared with medical masks in healthcare workers.

Conclusion: cloth or non-medical masks increase the risk of infection.

- https://www.ncbi.nlm.nih.gov/pmc/articles/PMC4420971/?fb clid=IwAR0IG6I0m4LAodUrP8ylmCbZRat9GSHTp73Wl E8_CfncjUprvPqObLo3qnI

These 12 Graphs Show Masks Do Nothing to Stop Covid

- https://thefederalist.com/2020/10/29/these-12-graphs-show-mask-mandates-do-nothing-to-stop-covid/

Alternative Treatments for Covid

Another piece to the deception puzzle is the smear of any and all alternative treatments. In order to create more chaos and steer us towards their solution, they had to destroy such treatments. Furthermore, they are censoring any doctors who are talking about Hydroxychloroquine, Ivermectin, Vit D, Zinc, and Monoclonal Antibodies. The first one we want to address is the smear of hydroxychloroquine. Somehow, they were able to get the *Lancet* (the world's most reputable peer-reviewed scientific journal) to print a categorically false study. Even though they retracted this article, the damage had been done.

- https://www.nbcnews.com/health/health-news/lancet-retracts-large-study-hydroxychloroquine-n1225091

Later we would find out that hydroxychloroquine and azithromycin therapy improved survival rates versus respirators by nearly 200%. Wouldn't that have been nice to know when they were hooking up all those people on respirators in New York? Instead, they fired doctors for prescribing it. Additionally, the internet and social media have blocked any content that included these helpful medications. Remember, if you create a problem that can be solved by a solution other than the one you want, you must suppress or smear it. Here are some other articles showing the censorship of promising forms of treatment, including chlorine dioxide, monoclonal antibodies, ivermectin, and vitamins.

- https://www.news-medical.net/news/20210602/HydroxychloroquineAzithromycin-therapy-at-a-higher-dose-improved-survival-by-nearly-20025-in-ventilated-COVID-patients.aspx

- https://pubmed.ncbi.nlm.nih.gov/33042552/

- https://drive.google.com/file/d/1AX2IOOP2CnOEFE 9mfcspV_Mf96Ra76pU/view

- https://www.fda.gov/news-events/press-announcements/coronavirus-covid-19-update-fda-authorizes-monoclonal-antibodies-treatment-covid-19-0

- https://combatcovid.hhs.gov/hcp/resources?utm_ source =mitregoogle&utm_medium=paidsearch&utm_campaign=futurelooksbright5122021&utm_content=Covid19_GP&utm_term=Englishhttps://www.citizensjournal.us/covid-deaths-plunge-after-major-world-city-introduces-ivermectin/

Big Tech Is Censoring Science Because COVID-19 Panic Made Them Rich

- https://thefederalist.com/2021/04/13/big-tech-is-censoring-science-because-covid-19-panic-made-them-rich-and-destroyed-their-competition/

Feds on Vitamins and Covid: Shut Up or Pay Up!

More lunacy from the federal government as they threaten doctors with $10,000 fines if they tell their patients the science about how vitamins and minerals can help with Covid.

- https://anh-usa.org/feds-on-vitamins-and-covid-shut-up-or-pay-up/

The Untreatable Myth

Dr. Peter A. McCullough is one of the most qualified Covid doctors in the world. Dr. McCullough's credentials include being "an internist, cardiologist, epidemiologist, Professor of Medicine at Texas A&M College of Medicine, President at the Cardiorenal Society of America, Editor-in-Chief of Cardiorenal Medicine and of Reviews in Cardiovascular Medicine, and a Senior Associate Editor at American Journal of Cardiology. He both practices medicine and publishes academic scientific studies."

Dr. McCullough is quick to point out that there has been a complete blockage with respect to any kind of treatment for Covid. We've been cut off because we are not allowed to know what other countries are doing, which is why we think Covid is untreatable unless the person is vaccinated. Instead, there is only one doctor that anybody has ever seen. Dr. McCullough talked about how he was lecturing on groundbreaking treatments for Covid that were the results of peer-reviewed scientific research, and yet he was dropped from YouTube for false information.

Like the doctors from the "Great Barrington Declaration," Dr. McCullough believes herd immunity is only attainable naturally because it is "complete and durable." He says that there is no rationale for ever being tested or vaccinated once you have already had Covid. He also mentions a study indicating that Texas may already have 80% herd immunity. He then goes on to reference a Chinese and British statement referencing the idea that "there's no such thing as asymptomatic spreader." Finally, Dr. McCullough says that he was part of some research in Texas that treats people before they go to the hospital. This research is so promising, he says they could reduce Covid deaths by 85%.

• https://www.youtube.com/watch?v=QAHi3lX3oGM

In another interview, Dr. Peter McCullough goes on to say that "COVID shots are obsolete, dangerous, and must be shut down." McCullough highlighted "five key messages of scientific truth" surrounding the pandemic that need to be taken into account:

45

1. The virus doesn't spread among asymptomatic people.
2. Asymptomatic people should not get tested, as it is "generating false positives, creating extra cases."
3. Natural immunity gained after having the virus is "robust, complete, and durable."
4. COVID-19 and even the variants are easily treatable at home with early intervention.
5. The coronavirus jabs by Pfizer, Moderna, Johnson & Johnson, and AstraZeneca "right now are obsolete."

Now let's look at why we are getting false positives from Covid testing.

- https://www.lifesitenews.com/blogs/top-american-doctor-covid-shots-are-obsolete-dangerous-must-be-shut-down/

The COVID-19 PCR Test

Early on in the Covid story, I was taught very quickly by the nurses coming into my office that the Covid test was inaccurate. They routinely talked about how they would go back and forth, testing negative and positive for months. Then the hospitals changed the protocol. If they tested positive, they were out for 10-12 days and allowed to return with no further testing. When 80% of the people testing positive have no symptoms, not only have they created hysteria, but these cannot be accurate. If our accountant or our doctor was only right 20% of the time, how many of us would keep them?

- https://time.com/5842669/coronavirus-asymptomatic-transmission/

More importantly, how can a test this inaccurate still be holding us all hostage? Is it any wonder why Bill Gates and George Soros bought the one test that controls everything?

- https://nationalfile.com/cdc-declares-pcr-tests-must-go-immediately-after-george-soros-bill-gates-buy-covid-19-test-manufacturer/

Yet, the world has never questioned the accuracy of this test. Instead, they came up with something never before considered in medicine, which is the idea of an asymptomatic carrier. Previously, we have never blamed someone with no symptoms for killing someone's grandmother, and the idea is still ludicrous. Not only is the RT-PCR test inaccurate, it cannot differentiate between an active or inactive virus or the flu.

Even the inventor of the PCR test, Nobel Peace Prize winner Dr. Kary Mullis, specifically stated that,

> The PCR test was never designed to tell you if you are sick. In the PCR, if you do it well, you can find almost anything in anybody... to make a whole lot of something out of something. It doesn't tell you... that the thing you ended up with really was going to hurt you or anything like that.

Even Fauci admits that most PCR tests are not done properly, which equals lots of false positives. Essentially, they are finding dead nucleotides and not infectious viruses. Fauci says anything above 35 cycles (other experts say just 30) is just dead nucleotides. Yet, the FDA has approved up to 40+ cycles. Too many cycles lead to 97% false positives. Not only does the video (link below) cover these facts, it also explains why we shouldn't take this supposed vaccine in one of the most clear and easy to understand presentations that even your kids could understand.

- https://www.bitchute.com/video/Juw4mI0Nmgr0/

Additionally, the FDA admits the Covid PCR test was developed without isolated Covid samples for test calibration, effectively revealing that it's testing something else.

- https://www.planet-today.com/2021/08/fda-document-ad-mits-covid-pcr-test-was.html#gsc.tab=0

Indeed, the Covid test itself is part of the disinformation warfare that they are using to bring us all under their control. The other problem with the test is it cannot differentiate between a live virus and an attenuated (non-infectious) virus. This is how they have effectively *increased the case numbers* to drive the pandemic narrative. Of course, what hospital will complain when every Covid diagnosis puts more money in the bank?

Though the whole world relies on RT-PCR to diagnose Sars-Cov-2 infection, the science is clear: they are not fit for the purpose (see below). Knowing this is a lie will expose the plan of Satan. Unfortunately, I have come to believe that an even bigger agenda has finally been revealed. Enter the Covid vaccine, which will soon be mandatory!

- https://bpa-pathology.com/covid19-pcr-tests-are-scientifi-cally-meaningless/

The Covid Vaccine

Remember, there is no reason anyone should take an emergency use only vaccine if they have no emergency.

While vaccines can have significant beneficial value, they can also be used for great evil because they allow access to our bodies. If you don't think vaccines can be used for evil, then watch the movie *The Origin of Aids*. Aids has killed 85 million people worldwide. The astonishing thing about the Covid vaccine is that it has mRNA in it, which is the part of our genetic material that determines the actions of our cells. RNA is also used in recombinant DNA or gene therapy.

Essentially, this not-a-vaccine is overwriting our God-given RNA codes with man-made ones. Consequently, this supposed vaccine is more consistent with genetic therapy. Why on earth would fighting COVID-19 require treatment that changes our genetic material? Who would want to do that? Yet, both political parties are pushing it here in America. The only difference is that some of them want it to be mandatory.

Still, most of us have never heard any kind of actual discussion about this treatment. The vaccine narrative runs strong in this country. If there is a disease, we should get vaccinated. However, like any treatment, the first question any of us should ask ourselves is if we need it. This means we need to know the risk levels we just covered. For most of us with no risk of dying, then why should we be worried about getting sick for a few days? Besides, many epidemiologists and doctors regard these kinds of common illnesses as essential to developing a healthy immune system.

Do not believe it! Check out the "The Great Barrington Declaration," which we have previously mentioned. Yet, most people don't know one doctor that opposes this supposed vaccine. So, here are some facts to consider. First, this is an experimental treatment. It has not even been approved by the FDA for regular use because it does not meet the FDA's rigorous scientific standards (see below). Even more shocking is that when the Pfizer jab was supposedly FDA approved for normal use, it actually wasn't. **But something that wasn't even available yet was (Comirnaty).**

Unfortunately, this did not stop half of the companies in America from requiring it. All of this happened through an executive order that has allowed certain people to be treated while studies of safety and effectiveness are still ongoing. In other words, safety and effectiveness are still up in the air, which is why they are still experimental. What is also disturbing is that US officials have given vaccine makers complete indemnity against damages, which means they can't be sued.

- https://www.fda.gov/emergency-preparedness-and-response/coronavirus-disease-2019-covid-19/covid-19-vaccines

Furthermore, the vaccine does not protect you from catching Covid, nor does it prevent you from spreading Covid, which means the 90% effectiveness advertisement was a lie. According to the research trials, the vaccine only is effective in reducing the symptoms of Covid if you are infected. That is why they are stating that even if you are vaccinated, you will still need to continue to wear a mask and social distance.

Should Vaccines Be Made Mandatory?
Why are they bullying us?

- https://www.youtube.com/watch?v=bYKGXDm3a00& feature=youtu.be&fbclid=IwAR0VZzfLDa1IvCI7DNCR -X4q5OzJyP7ONTaEFBvSNqkCrwszeibho_y0NY4

Is something nefarious going on? Why are some people saying that the Bill Gates Foundation's COVID-19 vaccine is a Satanic Plot? (see below) I think it would be safe to say that Bill Gates wants to vaccinate and chip the whole world. Vaccines really could have nano-teched particles that allow us to be identified, tracked, and even genetically manipulated. Patent #060606 is only one of the technologies we will discuss later in Beast Technology.

- https://blockchain.news/news/bill-gates-foundations-covid-19-vaccine-is-satanic-plot-says-oscar-winner

The Fetal Tissue Issue

Fetal tissue is also a big issue when it comes to vaccines. Yet, most people are surprised that vaccines typically have any fetal tissue in them at all. Obviously, this is a huge issue for Christians and one we need to continue to take before the court of public opinion. Fortunately, most people are still sympathetic to the plight of the unborn child.

CDC Admits That Vaccines Have Fetal Tissue:

- https://www.cga.ct.gov/2020/phdata/tmy/2020HB-05044-R000219-Wrinn%2015,%20Chris-TMY.PDF

Abortion Opponents Protest COVID-19 Vaccines' Use of Fetal Cells

- https://www.sciencemag.org/news/2020/06/abortion-opponents-protest-covid-19-vaccines-use-fetal-cells

Unfortunately, some articles will deny the use of fetal tissue in vaccines. The worst one I found asks the question and then tells us that it is a big no. Then they go on to say that vaccines use fetal tissue that is 60 years old. Now, how is 60-year-old fetal tissue still not fetal tissue? They also say that this fetal tissue was legally and electively aborted in the early 1960s. Do you see the denial? This is why one of the greatest strategies for us as Christians is to break the deception and to continue to represent the interest of the unborn. (See: Pfizer Whistleblower leaks e-mails on fetal cells.)

While I do not want to get sidetracked on abortion, I do want to give enough pause to list why I believe this is a crucial issue. First, child sacrifice was a part of the worship of false pagan gods. Stevie Nicks, not to single her out, tells us that if she hadn't had her abortions, then we wouldn't have had Fleetwood Mac. What that tells me is that Stevie worships the false gods of money, fame, and career. They are more important than children, and this is exactly how we have parented our generation—like they don't matter.

Second, we have politicians throwing parties and lighting up buildings in New York City to celebrate the ability to kill an infant the day before their due date. This is one of the most horrifying things I can imagine. They also support partial-birth abortions, the most barbaric thing still done on the planet. I don't know anyone who could watch the procedure, let alone perform one. All of this reveals that there really are monsters among us.

At the very least, a new holocaust of abortion is taking place on our watch. Now they want to make abortion part of our national health care to make us all accomplices. The question now becomes how can God not judge us for it. The next question is, why is it a problem to inject fetal tissue into our bodies? Hang with me for a second. The Passover is one of the most important festivals in the Bible because it was part of the Old Testament plan of salvation. Part of the Passover involved killing a lamb, ingesting it into their bodies, and then applying its blood to the doorpost of your house so that the angel of death would pass over.

Later, during the Passover supper, Jesus (the real Lamb of God) initiates the first communion with His disciples. Jesus breaks the bread, passes around the wine, and asks them to eat. By doing this, they are symbolically applying the body and the blood of Christ to their lives. So, what is happening when we take actual fetal tissue into our bodies? How are we not participating in some kind of unholy communion? So, in some sense, we became an accomplice and a participant in the shedding of this child's innocent life.

We could also say that we were marked because something was physically applied to our lives or made to be part of us. If it is the testimony of the blood of the Lamb that we must apply to our lives, then how is this not the opposite? Remember the Catholics believe that when they take communion, the wafer/wine literally becomes the blood and body of Jesus Christ. Shockingly, this too is the blood and body of a cloned fetus from the 1960s.

While the Covid vaccines are said to be free of fetal tissue, both Pfizer and Moderna did use fetal tissue in testing the vaccines. These are called fetal cell lines, and they don't consider them to be fetal tissue for the reasons we have discussed. They consider them to be immortalized cells cloned fetal tissue. However, they are still using fetal tissue to their benefit, and that is more than enough to say no to this vaccine for many of us.

Natural Immunity Versus mRNA Genetic Therapy

While we are being told every day all day long to take a vaccine, what is the difference between natural immunity versus vaccinated immunity?

Natural Immunity	Supposed Vaccine
If you are under 50 and have no underlying health condition, you have virtually no risk of dying from Covid.	If you are over 65 and have underlying conditions, then Covid is a more significant risk.
Natural immunity has kept us here for thousands of years.	50% of all vaccines have been pulled due to complications. Long term risk of mRNA therapy is unknown.
80% of those testing positive never have any symptoms.	50-80% of those who take genetic therapy get symptoms.
Provides robust & long-lasting immunity	Provides no immunity
Cannot transmit Covid	Can still transmit Covid
Immunity can last up to decades	Increased immunity is temporary.
100% natural	Experimental - there are no FDA approved vaccines available.
Maintains my God-given genetic coding	Not a vaccine. This is genetic therapy that overwrites my God-given RNA codes and makes my body produce spike proteins, which is a pathogen that makes people sick.
Safe because natural immunity survival rates are extremely high: Age / Survival Rate 0-14 / 99.9998% 15-44 / 99.9931% 45-65 / 99.9294% 65-85 / 99.6297% Over 85 / 98.2499%	Not Safe – CDC listed side effects are too numerous to count. No long-term testing on human or animals. No testing on pregnant patients. No testing on brain, kidneys, lungs, or heart. No testing on the effects on our DNA. No testing on pre- or post-natal development. Includes experimental ingredients, industrial chemicals, and "proprietary" ingredients, which means they won't tell us what it is.
No liability needed.	Prep Act Makes Insurance companies not liable.
Works Well	Does not work

Once people understand their personal risk level, most people under 65 with no underlying health conditions can see why natural immunity is the best choice. Instead, people are bullied into getting this experimental vaccine, which is a crime against humanity. Overvaccinating a population during a pandemic is also dangerous. Like overusing anti-biotics, we can create super strains. Interesting, many are blaming the unvaccinated for the new variants, but natural immunity has never been accused of this before.

Vaccines Don't Work

With all of this pressure and constant 24/7 dialog about how we all need to take this supposed vaccine, vaccines don't even work. At the time of the final editing of this book, Covid cases are going through the roof, and all of the liberal politicians want to shut everything down and make us wear masks again. But as of this week, 70% of the adult population in the United States have received at least one dose of a COVID-19 vaccine.

- https://www.kff.org/coronavirus-covid-19/issue-brief/latest-data-on-covid-19-vaccinations-race-ethnicity/

This is the intelligence test of our lifetime, and America is failing. It doesn't matter what they show on TV; we cannot have an epidemic of Covid when 70% of adults are vaccinated unless the vaccine does not work. As we have seen, children are not at risk of dying from Covid, so why are they being held hostage or threatened with vaccination? People are losing their jobs and being unfriended for not taking something that is useless. While the CDC was initially manipulating data to prop up "vaccine effectiveness," the cat is now out of the bag.

- https://off-guardian.org/2021/05/18/how-the-cdc-is-manipulating-data-to-prop-up-vaccine-effectiveness/

- https://www.infowars.com/posts/caught-red-handed-cdc-

changes-test-thresholds-to-virtually-eliminate-new-covid-
cases-among-vaxxd/

Consequently, many are now warning that Pfizer/Moderna
vaccines don't provide immunity against Covid. Meanwhile, they
were advertising 90% effectiveness with the supposed vaccines. But
it doesn't matter, they could say anything and still have no liability.
The surges we are seeing in the US also happened in Chile despite
having 60% of the population vaccinated, but no one took notice.

- https://www.forbes.com/sites/joewalsh/2021/04/06/covid-
  is-surging-in-chile-despite-high-vaccination-rates—-
  heres-why-the-us-should-take-notice/?sh=1906df49b6c7

Consequently, there are only two possibilities for this spike in
Covid cases. Either the Covid test is inaccurate, or the vaccine
doesn't work. Which lie works for you? Furthermore, a CDC study
showed that 74% of people infected in Massachusetts were fully
vaccinated. Similar results are found in Israel, indicating the vaccinated comprise the majority of the deaths.

- https://www.cnbc.com/2021/07/30/cdc-study-shows-
  74percent-of-people-infected-in-massachusetts-covid-out-
  break-were-fully-vaccinated.html?__source=sharebar%7Cf
  acebook&par=sharebar&fbclid=IwAR3NzckpIZlV9CtWe
  CjlN1SlsGOVUaPWQ1cXLXCnb52rGXKIwNNUAeH
  TRpk

- https://www.google.com/amp/s/www.businessinsider.com/
  israel-50-of-delta-variant-cases-vaccinated-severe-2021-
  6%3famp

Concurrently, we find out that Covid has infected about 100
vaccinated crewmembers on the HMS Queen Elizabeth.
Meanwhile, I have had to cancel my cruise because I won't take a
vaccine. Essentially, I am considered infectious.

- https://www.foxnews.com/world/covid-19-infects-about-100-vaccinated-crewmembers-on-royal-navys-hms-queen-elizabeth-report:

A study published by the NIH showed reduced effectiveness of several vaccines on the Delta variant with respect to antibody neutralization. "Sera (serum – fluids) from individuals who had received one dose of the Pfizer or the AstraZeneca vaccine had a barely discernible inhibitory effect on the Delta variant."

- https://pubmed.ncbi.nlm.nih.gov/34237773/

All of these contradictions are glaring. Either this works, or it doesn't. But at this point, anyone listening to the mainstream media has to be starting to wake up and say that everything they are doing is making it worse. Even the most liberal of pundits, Michael Rapaport is asking with expletives, "Figure this **** out!' Am I a Hero or a Super Spreader?"

- https://www.bizpacreview.com/2021/07/29/vaccinated-lefty-actor-lit-into-fauci-figure-this-sh-out-am-i-a-hero-or-a-super-spreader-1110633/

Unfortunately, they are all now attacking the one population that has resisted them. The unvaccinated are now deemed to be to blame for everything, including the new Delta variant. As a result, they must be discriminated against and labeled. This is the fight of our lifetime. Remember, once Hitler marked the Jews and began disenfranchising them, it was all over. The same is true of the vaccine passports.

As far as the new Delta variant, there is no test for it. Furthermore, as we will see when we get to chapter 8, the coronavirus was man made. Consequently, if so, then what is the most likely explanation of the second version? My opinion about the Delta variant is that they had to have it to cover up the fact that the vaccine didn't work. No matter whether there is a new variant or not, the vaccine isn't working, which means that America must stop listening to the false prophets.

The Slandering of Natural Immunity

On June 23, 2021, Kentucky Senator Rand Paul at the Senate Health Committee hearing stated that the majority of false claims about natural immunity being less effective protection against future Covid infections were coming from the government. He questioned former President of the America Medical Association (Dr. Susan Bailey) on COVID-19 vaccinations and why the government is spreading misinformation about peer-reviewed sources stating natural immunity is as effective, if not more effective, against Covid as vaccines. But this is not the only expert stating the obvious that natural immunity is superior to vaccinated immunity.

• https://youtu.be/ogA-U3Fy6ww (note: link to clip)

Dr. Ben Edwards is a medical expert who has testified before the Senate Committee on State Affairs about how unusual all of the medical reactions to Covid have been, especially compared to other vaccines in history. Dr. Edwards also talks about how preposterous it is to have someone vaccinated when they already have natural immunity. Sadly, naturally immune people also have a two to three times higher chance of having adverse reactions to the supposed vaccine. The beautiful thing is that Dr. Edwards states that when it comes to such things, he trusts in God and his body. Dr. Edwards also renounced the spirit of needless fear proclaimed over this nation.

• https://www.youtube.com/watch?v=60VGiW0cXDc

Here are four studies on natural immunity. The first one is another banned paper where doctors perform a risk-versus-benefit assessment of Covid jabs. The doctors also do a systematic and thorough review of how natural immunity is superior, and vaccines are unnecessary. The second study also found that natural immunity after Covid was durable and robust. The third study, published by the CDC, showed the persistence of SARS-CoV-2 antibodies in children six months after having Covid. Finally, the last study shows that natural immunity is durable and broad in resisting SARS-CoV-2 infection with persisting antibody responses and memory B and T cells. Their conclusion: "Taken together, these results suggest that broad and effective immunity may persist long-term in recovered COVID-19 patients."

- https://thetruthiswhere.wordpress.com/2021/05/18/banned-paper-doctors-risk-versus-benefit-assessment-of-covid-jabs/

  https://www.precisionvaccinations.com/natural-immunity-after-covid-19-found-durable-and-robust

  https://wwwnc.cdc.gov/eid/article/27/8/21-0965_article

  https://pubmed.ncbi.nlm.nih.gov/33948610/

(In Israel) Nearly 40% of new COVID patients were vaccinated compared to just 1% who had been infected previously.

- https://www.israelnationalnews.com/News/News.aspx/309762

- https://sharylattkisson.com/2021/08/report-israel-vaccination-provides-far-less-protection-than-previous-covid-infection/

Essentially, the powers that be are slandering natural immunity, but that would change everything we have ever known about immunity because it is always the most effective. Remember, God's ways are higher than ours. Vice versa, it would seem difficult to believe that a few scientists can do a better job of writing our mRNA than God can. Consequently, as for me and my house, I'm going to go with God on this one. However, before we go any deeper into the Covid narrative or the supposed vaccine, we must go back to the Bible to see if there is something prophetic happening here. More importantly, are all of these things a sign of the return of Jesus or the coming of the mark of the beast?

The Difference Between Love and Hate

The way to tell the difference between love and hate is that while love can never agree with hate, it always allows hate to have a choice. But when hate begins to take our choices and our freedoms away, love can no longer stay quiet because love cannot exist without freedom.

It must be time for some encouragement. Already, I feel heavy with the weight of all this information. It has caused me many sleepless nights, and I have had to pray for God to return to me "the joy of my salvation" on many occasions. Most importantly, this information is polarizing for everyone who hears it one way or the other. But this is not my goal. I do not want to offend anyone, but I also must stand for the truth. In that process, I have tried numerous ways to communicate these truths and failed. Recently God gave me a word picture to help explain why I cannot go along with this any longer.

Above all things, we know that God is love. Unfortunately, most of us don't know human love, much less perfect love. It is the lack of knowing love that has caused me a lot of confusion regarding what to do in this situation. Yet, most people think love just accepts everything, instead of standing for something. If perfect love lets hate inside its door, then it would no longer be perfect love. Essentially, if love lets hate in, love is hating itself. The same is true of us. We cannot let hate in, but we can offer hate a choice. But if hate cannot be convinced, love cannot sit idly by and watch hate destroy the ones it loves.

The way to know who is who in our world today is by the freedom of choices that they allow. When I share with my patients the quote above, they seem to understand. Mandates are simply not what love would do. If someone believes their mask or vaccine works, then why will they not give us the choice about whether we want to wear or take one? If our bodies really are our temple, then they are sacred. Allowing access to our bodies is our ultimate freedom. Indeed, the only thing that will turn this situation around is love, and that is what we must try and wake up inside of ourselves and in everyone who will listen.

3

Satan's Ultimate Weapon

What Is the Mark?

Before we talk about the connections of the mark of the beast (MOB), and the current Covid vaccine, I want to explore the MOB, in general, to see if we can narrow things down just a bit. The problem is that this is tough to do. While speculation sounds pointless, this is what we are forced to do because this mark is the greatest mystery of the Bible. More importantly, if we could get ahead of this, millions of people could be saved. So, please take this chapter with a grain of salt, but I believe it will still be worth it.

I am not trying to say that I know what the MOB is, but I am also pointing out that you probably don't either. Unfortunately, even my preconceived ideas about the MOB could end up being part of the deception if I am wrong. This is why we do not assume anything. For example, many people think it will be a chip or a visible bar code, but those are so yesterday.

Still, the biggest problem I run into when I talk to people about the MOB is that they think it will be obvious. They don't believe there will be any deception surrounding the MOB. I hope they are right. Unfortunately, I see no biblical case to be made that during the greatest deception in human history, there will be absolutely no deception surrounding the one thing that will accomplish Satan's ultimate goal. Unfortunately, I just don't believe the MOB will be labeled the mark of the beast.

Furthermore, if the serpent tricked Eve into taking the forbidden fruit, why can't we believe that there will be some trickery surrounding Satan's next big temptation? Still, I hope they are right, but our purpose is to question everything so that we are not deceived. I realize that I might be describing a worst-case scenario. But my default philosophy on things like this is as follows: "Hope for the best and plan for the worst." The truth between the best case and the worst case may lie somewhere in the middle. The good news is that you get to decide what that is.

Many Christians have already decided how end time events will unfold. For example, we keep thinking that it is the beast government and the Antichrist (AC) that bring about the MOB, but what if it is the cause (we are about to describe) that makes everything possible and even forms the beast government? Then there is the mark itself. What could cause modern people to worship Satan? How did they not only lose their souls but also their minds as well? Yet, what is coming is not something that we can sit down and draw out. Indeed, preconceived timelines could be part of the larger deception.

What does seem apparent is that the mark is somehow intertwined with other developments during the last days of human history. Even if the AC institutes the final version of the MOB, that doesn't mean earlier versions don't lay all the groundwork. Reversing this order means that the one-world government and the AC will rise after the cause enters the world. This would make sense because all chaos can lead to control.

The timing of the rapture is another thing we don't know with certainty. Don't get me wrong; I am rooting for the easiest way out as well, but allowing some fluidity to end-time events is critical so that we do not lock ourselves into some kind of paradigm and end up missing the boat. The idea of some events having a precursor also makes sense. After all, the first rocket we built did not get someone on the moon, and this may be true of the MOB. If the MOB is technology-related, then keep in mind virtually no technology has ever rolled out in its perfected state. But mark my words, it will be hard to deny that something just went up in the air.

This precursor to the MOB may do nothing more than get us used to giving up access to our bodies. However, just because this isn't the MOB, doesn't mean it isn't a crime against humanity or that it won't be harmful. It could be "one small step for mankind" before the giant leap that causes us to lose our humanity. Just implementing these mandates alone could allow them to strip every Christian of their job and possessions, thereby removing them from power and influence in our society.

For my money, the MOB should be considered the pinnacle of Satan's deception since it accomplishes his ultimate goal, which is obtaining the soul of everyone who takes it. At that point, isn't forming a beast kingdom, taking complete control, and being worshiped just formalities? Frankly, it will be difficult to miss the rise of a one-world government and its charismatic leader (the Anti-christ).

That would be like missing the advent of both the Roman Empire and Caesar at the same time. But identifying the MOB is the puzzle within the puzzle. Nonetheless, I believe the precedent we can set for Christians is that we should be wary of worldwide causes or dilemmas that allow big governments and their leaders to mandate their need to have access to our bodies in any way. Remember, the MOB is coming, and with it, there is a fundamental change in how we will need to preach the gospel.

The Precursor

While we have been debunking the Covid narrative and laying the groundwork to understand the ethical problems with vaccines, we now want to talk about how the vaccines directly connect to the mark of the beast. But before we get going too far, I want to say a few things to put my readers at ease. First, we are still living in the age of grace, and there is still time to right the ship. All of salvation is still available to us, but it is also time to wake up. Indeed, the

63

church needs to stop being lukewarm because the world is in travail, and the nations are being shaken as we speak.

Second, I do not believe this supposed vaccine is the real MOB, but it could be if some of the other technology available today was put in it. Unfortunately, some of the ingredients to the vaccines are proprietary, meaning they will not reveal their "finger licking good recipe." So, there is no way of knowing exactly what is in them. However, I have come to believe that the Covid narrative is both a crime against humanity and, at minimum, the precursor to the MOB. More importantly, before we are finished, I believe you will agree with me that something is definitely afoot.

The Mark of the Beast

Lest Satan should get an advantage over us. For we are not ignorant of his devices (2 Corinthians 2:11).

To understand the coming deception, we must know Satan's ultimate goal. Most people would probably say that it is to steal our souls, and this would be quite accurate. Of course, Satan has been accomplishing this goal in a host of ways. Yet, no matter what we have done in this life, and as long as we are alive, God can still conquer every sin through the gospel of Christ. Essentially, Satan can never have us in such a way that God can't take us back.

But does Satan come up with a way of changing that equation? Can Satan fool some of us into choosing to do something that keeps us from being saved? After all, Adam and Eve were fooled into taking the forbidden fruit into their bodies even though God forewarned them not to eat it. Unfortunately, the Bible says that Satan comes up with another forbidden fruit—a way to nullify the gospel—but only if someone chooses to take the mark of the beast. This makes the MOB the ultimate deception and true agenda behind the greatest conspiracy Satan has ever crafted against God and His children.

The MOB doesn't mean that Satan wins because God has warned us about this situation over 2000 years ago. God is also not getting outsmarted because He has commanded us in the same way He did Adam and Eve not to put something into their bodies. Unfortunately, the church isn't hearing or sharing the warning, and some people have never even heard about it. In my heart, if this book accomplishes nothing more than getting us all talking about the MOB, then I believe that millions of people could be saved because of it. Now, if you are wondering how the MOB could do something like this, join the club.

I have also had the same question about exactly how "eating a fruit" could start this whole mess. But truly understanding God and the courts of heaven are above my pay grade. So I recommend learning to accept the explicit directions of God when it comes to this area instead of our own reasoning. Now is not the time to start trusting human reasoning, our governments, or technology. Now is the time to trust and obey the One who has brought us this far to trust that what He started within us, He is fully able to finish (2 Timothy 1:12).

For as the heavens are higher than the earth, so are My ways higher than your ways, And My thoughts than your thoughts (Isaiah 55:9 NKJV).

The Beast Passages

This thwarting of the gospel is why I believe the MOB represents the greatest mystery because it is the one thing that we cannot repent of once we have taken it. Consequently, let's just take a moment and review some of the key passages in the Bible talking about the MOB and why God gave us this stern warning.

Revelation 13:16-18 (KJV)

And he causes all, both small and great, both rich and poor, both free and slave, to be marked on the right hand or the forehead, so that no one can buy or sell unless he has the mark, that is, the name of the beast or the number of its name. This calls for wisdom: let the one who has understanding calculate the number of the beast, for it is the number of a man, and his number is 666.

Revelation 14:9-11 (KJV)

And another angel, a third, followed them, saying with a loud voice, "If anyone worships the beast and its image and receives a mark on his forehead or his hand, he also will drink the wine of God's wrath, poured full strength into the cup of his anger, and he will be tormented with fire and sulfur in the presence of the holy angels and in the presence of the Lamb. And the smoke of their torment goes up forever and ever, and they have no rest, day or night, these worshipers of the beast and its image, and whoever receives the mark of its name."

Revelation 20:4 (NKJV)

Then I saw thrones, and seated on them were those to whom the authority to judge was committed. Also, I saw the souls of those who had been beheaded for the testimony of Jesus and for the word of God, and those who had not worshiped the beast or its image and had not received its mark on their foreheads or their hands. They came to life and reigned with Christ for a thousand years.

Revelation 19:20 (BSB)

But the beast was captured, and with it the false prophet who had performed the signs on its behalf. With these signs he had deluded those who had received the mark of the beast and worshiped its image. The two of them were thrown alive into the fiery lake of burning sulfur."

These verses are not a lot to go on. Consequently, while there are a few things we know about the mark of the beast, there is more we don't know. Here are a few of the things that stand out.

1. We know that everyone who gets the MOB is motivated by some unknown situation or cause driving everyone toward the MOB. In this sense, the MOB seems to be a solution to this cause. The universal nature of the cause also appears to produce the greatest peer pressure situation in human history.

2. We know that our governments will need physical access to our bodies to deal with this situation, and it will eventually be mandatory.

3. We know that they are going to mark us in some way. Based on current technology, the mark will probably be invisible, most likely nanotechnology or genetic markers.

4. There will be consequences to not taking this mark, but we have to choose it. At first, we will not be able to buy or sell. How democratic, right? But later, some souls were beheaded for not taking this mark.

5. If we take this mark, then we cannot be saved.

6. The mark has something to do with our right hand and/or our forehead, which we will discuss at length.

7. There may be a connection of this mark to the number of man, which is the number 666.

8. The people who take this mark will also worship the beast and its image.

In the end, we will win! The beast and the false prophet will be thrown into the lake of fire, while those who did not take the mark will reign with Christ for 1000 years.

What Kind of Mark?

We have previously addressed the fact that many modern technologies would be invisible to the eye but visible on a scanner. The most prominent placement for scanning someone would be either their right hand or their forehead. Now think about it as if you were someone from 2000 years ago observing the situation. The only people allowed to move about freely had their right hand or their forehead scanned with modern technology. Coincidentally, sometime in the past year, most of us have had our foreheads scanned for our temperature prior to being allowed to enter a place of business. This observation alone tells us that "things are beginning to happen." But, as we will see, both the system and technology for the MOB are already here.

The Unforgivable Sin

Why did I say that the MOB will change the gospel we are called to preach? The Bible says that if you take the MOB, then you cannot be saved. What Jesus did on the cross was previously able to redeem all the sins of all humanity. Yet, somehow Satan comes up with something new, a new forbidden fruit, and now salvation no longer applies to them. What could possibly do something like this? What has changed so drastically?

If we cannot be saved once we take the mark of the beast, then the gospel we preach in the last days must be updated to reflect this change. Consequently, we must begin to preach against the MOB right away and with as many details as possible. Essentially, the game has changed. We may still be playing football, but Satan has just driven a tank out onto the field. The idea that the MOB destroys the ability of the gospel to save people is shocking. Especially when previously, no matter what a human does in their lifetime, God can still redeem them if they repent and turn to Christ. But there is one exception to this, which is called "blaspheming the Holy Spirit."

Truly I say to you, all sins shall be forgiven the sons of men, and whatever blasphemies they utter; but whoever blasphemes against the Holy Spirit never has forgiveness, but is guilty of an eternal sin—because they were saying, "He has an unclean spirit" (Mark 3:28-30 BSB).

Remember, all that is needed for the power of the gospel to work is for us to confirm the testimony of Christ and repent. Our spirit bears witness with the Holy Spirit to bring us into alignment with Jesus. Then the Holy Spirit can begin to intercede for us. In the process, we receive a new revelation of our citizenship in heaven because of our new relationship with God Himself. Exactly, what could thwart this?

Again, technology is one of the best explanations of why Satan doesn't pull out this trump card much earlier. Consequently, we will be discussing a lot of technology very soon. Maybe the MOB just wasn't possible before this point in human history. One of the last things I will say about the imminent need for preaching about the MOB has to do with the rapture. Because some of us will be gone does not mean that there will be no one left behind, which means what we preach now will be all they have to go on.

Even the timing of the rapture is not 100% set in stone. Yet, no one has ever told us that we could all one day be in a situation where we have to say no to something that isn't even labeled mark of the beast. Our preconceived ideas about the timing of end time events could be setting people up for failure. Again, part of my premise is there could be more deception about the MOB than anything else in history. Consequences could be grave, as many will be forced to have to give up their lives, or at least their ability to buy and sell, in order to avoid this mark. This is the kind of knowledge that will keep us from perishing.

My people are destroyed for lack of knowledge. Because you have rejected knowledge, I will also reject you as My priests. Since you have forgotten the law of your God, I will also forget your children (Hosea 4:6 NKJV).

Because the end times represent the greatest peer pressure situation in history, we need to prepare as many people as possible. My favorite strategy for dealing with peer pressure is given by Dr. James Dobson. Dr. Dobson lays out a situation that most of us have already experienced. We get into a car where everyone is smoking, drinking, or taking drugs. Dr. Dobson says that your children will take whatever is offered unless two things have already happened: First, they have been told that one day they will be offered one of these things. Second, the children must have decided ahead of time what they will say when that happens. These days, it is not a matter of if.

Consequently, our expectations about the MOB and end-time events are important. Essentially, false expectations can end up destroying us, but realistic expectations can lead us to life. We don't have to be dogmatic about when, where, and how everything happens, but we do need to notice when biblical things are happening. Remember, in a free and open society, we should all be allowed to have conversations like this without everyone getting offended and leaving the church. After all, there is no condemnation to those who are in Christ.

At the same time, ignoring that there is a new cause in the world and the incredible fear it is creating is not something we can ignore. At least that is what I thought until I realized our pastors aren't talking about this. But I can't change what time it is, and you can't either. Even though things will get shaken, our attitude and our mantra should still be "no fear."

God has not given us a spirit of fear, but of power and of love and of a sound mind (2 Timothy 1:7 NKJV)

A Deeper Dive into Revelation 13:16

He causes all, both small and great, rich and poor, free and slave, to receive a mark on their right hand or their foreheads (KJV).

The Cause - (Greek Word 4160) - Every cause has an effect—to make someone do something, which means there is a cause or chaos of some kind that pushes us towards a prescribed action or solution. "Cause" has been translated to execute, expose, form (a conspiracy), produce, or perform.

The Mark – (Greek Word 5480) - This word means to stamp, etch, impress, as in the case of a sculpture, a coin, a seal, branding, a die, or engraving. It can also be translated as something that provides undeniable identification, a symbol showing an irrefutable connection between two parties, an identification-marker, or an owner's unique brand-mark.

This form of marking could easily be fulfilled by genetic markers such as DNA or a host of other biometric technologies. The root word (deeper meaning) of "mark" is *charassó*, which means to sharpen or engrave (implying what makes the mark is sharp). Certainly, a syringe used to mark someone with its ingredients can fulfill this idea.

Right Hand or Side - (Greek Word 1188) - While this word means right hand or side, there is something about this word that has been lost in translation. Here are some verses with the same word.

If your right eye causes you to sin, pluck it out and cast it from you; for it is more profitable for you that one of your members perish, than for your whole body to be cast into hell (Matthew 5:29 NKJV)

Jesus said. "But to sit at My right or left is not Mine to grant. (Matthew 20:23 BSB)

Jack Wellman has written an article that talks about "What Does the Right Hand Symbolize or Mean in the Bible?" What is interesting is that God says, in Isaiah 41:13, "For I, the Lord your God, hold your right hand... Fear not, I am the one who helps you." Remember, anything God desires is also something that Satan desires. This taking or giving of right hand is reminiscent of walking along with God in the Garden of Eden because it implies a close relationship or belonging.

- https://www.patheos.com/blogs/christiancrier/author/jwellman/

Being in someone's right hand implies being under their authority and protection. "The Lord said to my Lord, 'Sit at my right hand, until I make your enemies your footstool'" (see Luke 20:42-43 and also Luke 22:69). Being in God's right hand also signifies the special place that we hold in God's heart. But what God holds in love, Satan holds in hate and condemnation. How fearful it must be to have Satan holding us in his hands and be marked by his signet.

The key to our "right hand" is to notice that we are probably not talking about something literal. The right hand seems to indicate a special place of honor and allegiance. Consequently, holding or marking our right hand appears to be akin to bridling a horse. Thus, it would appear that giving anything else but God our "right hand" is some form of idolatry. Indeed, this is what is happening with the MOB. Not being able to buy or sell also implies that we have not given Satan our right hand.

Hand - (Greek Word 5495) - The word properly means the hand, but figuratively, it can mean the instrument a person uses to accomplish their purpose, intention, or plan. It has been translated "agency, charge, and grasp." Essentially, if Satan marks our "hand," we could become his instrument to accomplish his plans. Satan marking our hand can also mean he has taken charge over us, and we are now in his grasp.

The Forehead - (Greek Word 3359) -

I thank God through Jesus Christ our Lord. So then with the mind, I myself serve the law of God; but with the flesh the law of sin (Romans 7:25).

The literal translation of this word is "after the eye," "behind the eyes," or possibly, "between the eyes." Obviously, what is between our eyes is the frontal lobe of the brain, which houses our mind, our speech, and our personality. A mark on our foreheads could represent a change to how we think, feel, or even what we perceive. According to occultism, the forehead is also the location of the "third eye," which we will cover in chapter six.

The root word for forehead is *Meta* – (Greek Word 3326). This word has a deeper meaning, which implies there has been a "change afterward" (i.e., what results after an activity); the after-effect (change or result) is defined by the context. Think of a butterfly going through a metamorphosis. Before the process, he is a caterpillar, but afterward, he is a butterfly.

Applying that to humans means before the process, you were a human being; but afterwards, you are something different—"a meta-human." The fact that this change takes place on our forehead implies that we go through a metamorphosis of the mind. Interestingly, DC Comics calls their superheroes "meta-humans," which is their term for a modified human being. Coincidence or not? We will delve deeply into this possibility.

An Expanded Translation of Revelation 13:16

Satan **causes** (G4160) and executes a plan, exposes a weakness, forms a conspiracy, produces chaos, and performs an Oscar-winning performance that affects everyone (small, great, rich, poor, old, young, slave, and free). In turn, people receive a **mark** (G5480), stamp, or etching, become a sculpture (made in a new image), are sealed, imprinted with a signet, branded with a die or engraving that "provides undeniable identification," a symbol showing an irrefutable connection between the two parties, an identification-marker, an owner's unique "brand-mark."

The root word "**mark**" (G5480) hints that the process will be carried out by something sharpened to a point, such as a needle. The mark is literal but may not be visible. However, the place we are marked, our **right hand** (G1188), is not necessarily a literal place because it mainly represents a particular part of us (what we value, trust; our power and authority) that only God, as our Father, has the right to hold (Isaiah 41:13). Because Satan now (figuratively or literally) holds our **hand** (G5495), it could mean he controls our purpose, intention, or plan, thereby thwarting God's plan, intention, and purpose.

This mark on our **foreheads** or "after (behind) the eyes" (G3359) could easily be referring to the frontal lobe of our brain, which contains our conscious mind and personality. In this sense, a seal or mark on our foreheads could represent ownership of our mind and possibly our soul. When we consider that, "with the mind, we serve the law of God; but with the flesh, the law of sin," losing our Christian minds would make us entirely controlled by sin, and in all likelihood, unredeemable.

Lastly, the root word for the **forehead** (G3326) is the word "meta," and it implies a "metamorphosis of the mind." This dramatic changing of the mind would also explain why all those that take the mark worship the beast. Indeed, after someone takes the MOB, they could be referred to as a meta-human, synonymous with hybrid human beings, super-soldiers, or D.C. Comics superheroes. Meta-humans also brings to mind the genetic narratives of the Bible, such as the "Days of Noah."

False Assumptions

At this point, I want to stop and fully acknowledge why many Christians and pastors will not even entertain the idea that a precursor (pattern or template) to the MOB is already here because of any of the following:

1. The rapture hasn't occurred yet, so this can't be the MOB.

2. The Antichrist is the one who comes up with the MOB, and he hasn't appeared yet.

3. The one-world government isn't here yet, so this can't be the MOB.

4. The mark of the beast has to be something that we know is the MOB. In other words, there can be no deception concerning what the MOB is or what it does to us.

5. The MOB must be a visible mark or a physical computer chip in our right hand or forehead. This vaccine does not do that, so it cannot be the MOB.

6. The MOB is about worship of the beast, and vaccines have nothing to do with worship.

The problem with all of these statements is that the Bible does not teach these exact scenarios, let alone a step-by-step process for exactly how things will go in the end times. Just reading the expanded meaning of Revelation 13:16 should have triggered some new ideas about what might happen. Sure, there are some probable scenarios, but there is no definitive timeline or sequence of events given in scripture. For example, while the rapture is going to happen, the timing of the event is hotly debated. I would not bet my life on any of them.

As I have said at the start, my philosophy for how to navigate these trying times is found in Luke 21. In that passage, Jesus tells us the end would come shortly after Jerusalem is no longer trodden down by the gentiles. This occurred in 1967, but only recently has Jerusalem become the capital of Israel. It has been almost 2000 years, but suddenly, God's time clock started ticking again. Then next thing Jesus says is, "When you see these things beginning to happen, stand up, lift up your head, for your redemption is drawing closer."

Not only are God's people in control over Jerusalem, but specific parts of the MOB scenario are happening right now, and very few are talking about it. These things are happening! Yet, the church has refused to alter its next sermon series because they fail to recognize the "signs of the times." Alarms should have been sounding off to wake people up that Jesus is coming soon. We should have also been looking for the cause that would come into the world to deceive many.

Unfortunately, the fact is that the Bible tells us so little about the MOB. Consequently, it is surprising that we have gotten so dogmatic about exactly how all of this is going to happen. Our preconceived ideas are why people can't see the fulfillment of Bible prophecy even though it is happening right in front of them. The false assumptions we have talked about have stood in our way of recognizing what is happening. We have not talked about what is happening, and so we have missed out on who is in on this cabal.

It cannot be a coincidence that we have a worldwide coordinated push to enslave the world with vaccine passports. Later, we will talk about who this cabal will be in chapter eight, which fits precisely. Still, this is why I have always taught that Bible prophecy was not given to us to predict the future. Prophecy was given so we can know that God knows the future or that the future is here because the recorded prophecy is actually happening.

But the most important characteristic of the end times is deception. Don't you think that our enemy knows the common or most popular scenarios being taught about Bible prophecy? Wouldn't he naturally try and avoid them so that he did not set off any alarms? This is why Bible prophecy is cryptic. God is going to give us broader and more general warnings so that we can recognize an infinite variety of Satan's plans. Too many specifics and Satan would just change his plans.

The Abomination of Desolation—
An Alternative View

*And this gospel of the kingdom will be preached in all the world
as a testimony to all nations, and then the end will come. So,
when you see standing in the holy place "the abomination of
desolation," described by the prophet Daniel* (Matthew 24:15-
16 BSB).

Here is a good example of how we are so locked into a particular view that we might miss the whole point. Many theologians
would argue that the abomination of desolation (AOD) must take
place before the MOB. While the AOD seems to be correlated to
the destruction of the temple, it also commonly thought that the
AOD takes place when the Antichrist gets control of Jerusalem
and sits inside the temple. Currently, the temple hasn't even been
rebuilt, so this alone becomes a question mark as to why the AOD
has to precede the MOB. I believe that Satan cannot sit anywhere
until the "opening of the Abyss," which we will explain later in
chapter six.

In essence, the opening of the Abyss is when the spirit of the
Antichrist is released and then allowed to go into the person who
will be the Antichrist. Consequently, the AOD doesn't appear to
happen until we get closer to the middle of the Tribulation. So, it
would also make sense that people are marked for possession before the opening of the Abyss. But here is an alternative perspective. Is the MOB a form of the AOD? Before the temple in
Jerusalem was destroyed, the veil of the Holy of Holies was rent
from top to bottom, which signifies that God no longer resides in
the temple of Jerusalem.

For the past 2000 years, the Holiest of Holies has been inside
our bodies because our bodies are the temples of the Holy Spirit.
Changing the plans, likeness, or measurements of God's temple is
considered blasphemy. Consequently, if the MOB defiled our

bodies in such a way that it allowed Satan to sit on the throne of our hearts, then the AOD and the MOB are the same thing. Not only does this alternative perspective on the AOD open up some new possibilities, it also opens up the idea that defiling our temple is what the MOB is really all about.

Of course, I am not saying that the AOD won't also occur in the temple in Jerusalem, but the true temple of the Holy Spirit is in our bodies. After all, when Jesus said, "Destroy this temple, and in three days I will raise it up," Jesus was talking about His body (John 2:19). So, essentially, there may be a double meaning regarding the AOD and exactly what Satan is going to defile when he sits there.

The Cause

Satan's master plan will be executed through some type of cause, chaos, or problem. This turmoil will create the fear necessary to drive the masses to the solution the beast government has prescribed, which will give the government access to our bodies. What could cause an entire population to give up access to their bodies willingly? This is where the idea of "order out of chaos" can certainly explain some things. After all, the chaos creates the fear necessary to create a herd mentality, when extreme peer pressure causes people to take what they have prescribed to solve the problem they created.

What is this cause? For as long as I can remember, I have heard that a pandemic may the best explanation. Create the disease and then magically come up with the cure. This probable scenario is why most of the people in our family have typically never been vaccinated. Now 16 months into COVID-19, the entire narrative fits this idea perfectly. More importantly, people who have no risk of dying are lining up to give access to their bodies to take an experimental therapy that is for emergency use only. The question is, what will we line up for next?

In astonishing fashion, the Covid narrative has accomplished what no other narrative ever has. It has produced a worldwide phenomenon that could make Satan's master plan a reality. Satan may now have unfettered access to our bodies, and everyone seems to be in on it. This is why I don't trust any government or politician. In case you haven't studied world history, every government has done to the people what it was designed to protect them against. The only One I do trust is God, and He has warned me about situations like these.

More importantly, my body is His temple, and I will not allow anyone to have access to it without my full consent and for very good reason. The idea that our government should have access to our bodies to inject whatever it wants, whenever it wants, is the ultimate loss of personal freedom. Those who oppose this agenda are made out to be some kind of crazy conspiracy theorists or someone so ignorant that they need to be sent to some kind of re-education (concentration) camp.

The Threat

The next thing we know about the MOB is that it will become mandatory. Then there is the curious ultimatum that if we do not comply with the mandate, we cannot buy or sell. They could've just said, "Do this, or we kill you." They could just hold us all down and force it on us, but they don't. Why? Interestingly enough, taking this mark has some kind of unwritten rule behind it because it must be our own choice. Almost like they are democratic or something. But I have come to realize we have to choose it for it to hold up in the court of heaven.

While they can't force us to take it, they can lie, manipulate, deceive, and threaten us. Already, New York and most of Europe have vaccine passports, which will not allow someone to buy, sell, or have a job without having a vaccine. There are no "religious, philosophical, or personal exemptions."

These same mandates are now being enforced on all health care workers because up to 50% of health care professionals (as of 4/21) have not taken the vaccine. Not only should this alarm Americans that something might be amiss, but the fact that the people who we trust to make our health care decisions cannot be trusted to make their own is complete hypocrisy. The penalty would mean that people could lose their license, job, or the ability to travel, go to a restaurant or store, which all qualify for not being "allowed to buy or sell." This is exactly the same as the penalty for not taking the mark of the beast.

All of this is very unlikely to be a coincidence. And so my prophetic radar has gone off, and I believe it is time to blow the alarm because things are starting to line up. Some kind of connection between the Covid narrative and Satan's final agenda clearly exists. As Christians, we must resist these kinds of controls, manipulations, and nefarious agendas. However, as we have learned from scripture, this soft-sell side of the mandate will eventually become a hard sell (Revelations 20:4).

So, here is what we have so far. We have a worldwide pandemic that isn't killing more people than last year in our country. Miraculously companies have instantly come up with a cure. Now they are saying we can't go back to normal until we all take it. The problem is that we have to give them access to our bodies to do it. However, the vaccine isn't a vaccine (as we will see), and it isn't even FDA approved but only labeled for emergency use, which means it's experimental. Now, remember, they are manipulating us all to do this even if we have no actual risk of dying from Covid. Moreover, why are they pushing this so hard?

All of this is why my MOB alarm has gone off, and I will not remain silent any longer. The rise of a systemic cause pushing 24/7 fear for over a year, along with the distinct fulfillment of key components of the MOB scenario, should have all of us on high alert. Still, the question remains, just what is the MOB, and how could this vaccine be connected to it?

Vaccine Passports

What a clever name for saying they are putting everyone who doesn't take this vaccine under house arrest. In fact, losing our job will eventually lead to them taking everything we have. This is how the spreading of lies and fear has now turned into hate! It has now accomplished its goal of dividing America even though natural immunity is better than vaccinated immunity, and probably more than 50% of us already have it.

But if someone's mask or vaccine works, then why do we have to take it? I had a patient in my office that did not believe you can even get natural immunity to Covid. Yet, one of the professors at Johns Hopkins believes that half of Americans already has natural immunity. Dismissing this idea is the biggest failure of medical leadership.

- https://www.infowars.com/posts/johns-hopkins-prof-half-of-americans-have-natural-immunity-dismissing-it-is-biggest-failure-of-medical-leadership/

Furthermore, the recent increase in the number of Covid cases has proven that these supposed vaccines do not give immunity or stop transmission. Essentially, the vaccinated have no advantage over the unvaccinated. So, why should there be a vaccine passport?

Previously, most of the media in Europe passed off vaccine passports as a "conspiracy theory," until they did it. Now even universities are requiring students to take the jab even though students are at the lowest risk.

- https://www.naturalnews.com/2021-06-16-europe-launches-covid-vaccine-passports-media-conspiracy-theory.html

- https://www.foxnews.com/us/university-virginia-uva-mandate-covid-vaccination

However, vaccine passports would be the end of America as we know it. They are even being used to deny someone's access to their children. But the exclusion is starting to go both ways, which means the unvaccinated are beginning to refuse admission and services to the vaccinated.

- https://odysee.com/@SergeantMajor'sTrutherInfo:2/ DOCTORS,-ALONG-WITH-MANY-STORES-AND-SERVICES-ARE-NOW-REFUSING-TO-ADMIT-THE-VACCINATED—2021-05-03—WIL-PA RANORMAL-(VIDEO):9

People are unfriending each other over this whole issue, as Eric Clapton and Jennifer Aniston can attest.

- https://www.theblaze.com/news/eric-clapton-musician-friends-gone-covid-vaccine?utm_source=theblaze-dailyAM&utm_medium=email&utm_campaign=Daily-N ewsletter_AM%202021-06-17&utm_term=AC-TIVE%20LIST%20-%20TheBlaze%20Daily%20AM

But when our government forces a business to scrutinize their customers, we know the new "gestapo" is almost in place.

- https://www.bizpacreview.com/2021/05/20/red-flags-as-oregon-forces-businesses-to-ask-for-vaccine-passports-from-customers-that-go-maskless-1077081/

Fortunately, governors like Ron DeSantis in Florida have banned vaccine passports, which means all we can do is flee from the states that are now totalitarian regimes.

- https://www.nytimes.com/2021/04/02/us/florida-vaccine-passport-desantis.html

4

The Beast and the Vaccine

The First Lie

Satan is the father of lies. As Christians, we must be willing to address his lies, or we can never thwart his agenda. The first lie we must address is that this vaccine is a vaccine when it is really genetic therapy. The second lie is that all of this will go away if everyone just takes it. But this vaccine does not make us immune to COVID-19. Even after taking any of the vaccines, we can still catch and spread Covid. Since the supposed vaccine has been used, the numbers of cases have gone up, not down. Consequently, they are reverting to all the controls that didn't work the first time. Exactly how is this going back to normal?

At best, vaccines will only lessen the symptoms, but with the admission of the need for a booster, the long-term effects now look grim. Unfortunately, the church has divorced itself from matters of the state because they too have believed the same lie the media is selling. This divorce has left us churchgoers alone and empty as we try and make some of the most difficult choices of our lives. The problem is, we will have to roll up our sleeves and capitulate for the lie. Now all they need is a biometric mark to tell who has had the vaccine, and who hasn't.

Experimental Genetic Therapy

While vaccines may have had some beneficial value in the past with things like polio, measles, mumps, and rubella, they can also be used for great evil. If you don't think vaccines can be used by evil, then watch the movie, *The Origin of Aids*. Aids has killed 85 million people worldwide, and all of it could be related to a vaccine. Additionally, the movie gives a lot of information about how vaccines are made and why they work.

What cannot be missed is that something is different about this supposed Covid vaccine. As we have said, it should more accurately be called gene therapy because it is the first time that scientists are rewriting our God-given genetic codes. If the hair on the back of your neck just stood up, you are not alone. One of the key articles outlining these facts comes from an interview with Dr. David Martin.

- https://www.westonaprice.org/podcast/its-gene-therapy-not-a-vaccine/?fbclid=IwAR0o-Cle7BHI_CN51dNvmvfk9A8edy1OLEcm-UawHqEUz EQgkKd64MJ5NqQ#.YBrWL3nBgTg.facebook

This information can also be found in the vaccine paperwork from both Moderna and Pfizer, but Dr. David Martin drops quite a few bombs about the Covid deception and the supposed vaccines. The first is that this is not a vaccine in any traditional sense. The word "vaccine" is only being used to sneak it past the public perceptions, as well as health exemptions and protocols. Here are some of the most striking statements from the interview.

1. No vaccine is in development for … SARS-CoV-2 virus. That doesn't exist … (It's part of) the propaganda war.

2. When asked if SARS-CoV-2 was "the virus" and COVID-19 was the disease. Dr. Marten responded, "COVID 19 is not a disease. It is a series of clinical symptoms … The illusion in February was that SARS-CoV-2 caused COVID-19. The problem … is that the majority of people who test positive … are not ill at all. The illusion that the virus causes a disease fell apart. That's why they invented the term "asymptomatic carrier."

3. Most of the people who have a positive test will never have a single symptom. Most of the people who have symptoms do not have positive tests.

4. The official numbers ... trapped across the screens ... are willfully lying ... A viral infection hasn't been documented in the majority of what is called cases.

5. "What is being touted as a vaccination" is not. There is no "attenuated or live virus or a fragment of an attenuated virus." There is no prevention "from transmitting the infection," which is what the "common definition of a vaccine is meant to do.'

6. The problem is that in the case of Moderna and Pfizer, this is not a vaccine. This is gene therapy. It's sending a strand of synthetic RNA into the human being and is invoking ... the creation of the S1 spike protein, which is a pathogen. It's a toxin inside of human beings ... it's making your body produce the thing that makes you sick ... A vaccine is supposed to trigger immunity. It's not supposed to trigger you to make a toxin.

7. This (vaccine) is not going to stop you from getting Coronavirus. It's not going to stop you from getting sick. In fact, on the contrary, it will make you sick far more often than the virus itself. What is the purpose of getting this vaccine or this gene manipulation as you call it? "The benefit is non-existent. (There are) both short-term and long-term risks of altering their RNA and DNA from exposure to this gene therapy."

8. We're being told to take a treatment for a disease we don't have ... using careful marketing manipulation and propaganda, calling these things vaccines for public health ...

We've been primed to accept that approach. That's the (vaccine) narrative everybody expects.

9. In Moderna's own SEC filings, they make it abundantly clear that their technology is a gene therapy technology. In their clinical trial, they've made it abundantly clear that they could not measure the presence or absence of the virus, and they could not measure the presence or the absence of the transmission of the virus. Every single thing that ... preys on the public understanding of what vaccination is, they explicitly said, "They're not doing that."

10. The fact of the matter is the PCR (Covid) test has never been approved as a diagnostic ... (but it does) reinforce a propaganda narrative. It doesn't tell you anything. I've interviewed Dr. Tom Cowan and Dr. Andy Kaufman, and they say the same thing. The person who came up with or developed the PCR test says that it's not to be used to diagnose anything.

11. People don't understand that if you lift the state of emergency, the whole house of cards falls.

12. "I will not touch a thing, and I will not allow my body to be invaded with a thing that has been developed in an unethical and illegal way. I am not going to let anybody have the opportunity to manipulate my genetic code. It's not going to happen. If that means that it comes at a cost of a having particular employer or a particular relationship or whatever else, my life happens to be worth more than that. We've been conditioned to fall into this trap, which is, "We might not be able to get on a plane." So, drive.

Essentially, Dr. Marten is saying this vaccine is not a vaccine; it is mRNA packaged in a fat envelope to deliver a medical device into our cells that will force our cells into producing a pathogen. It does this by overriding our natural genetic coding and replacing it with their codes. This not-a-vaccine produces synthetic pathogens; it does not produce immunity. However, of all the things Dr. Martin says, one particular line stands out, and I know because I have been saying it for the past 12 years in my Bible prophecy conferences.

"I am not going to let anybody have the opportunity to manipulate my genetic code (DNA). It's not going to happen." When I say this, I have pastors ask me, "Why is it a problem to change our DNA?" My short answer is, "because God wrote our DNA Himself. Our DNA is what gives us our identity. Our DNA contains the encoded information that makes us look like the image of our Father. If God did not write our DNA, then God would not be our Father, but someone else would."

The idea that the world governments have begun genetic manipulation upon the masses should trip everyone's alarm here. It is worth repeating that for as long as I can remember, I have heard how a pandemic was the most likely explanation for the worldwide cause that made everyone give up access to their bodies and take the MOB. Now consider, I have been thinking about the MOB my whole life and exactly what this could be. The most troubling aspect is why Jesus can't save someone with the MOB.

The best explanation I have come up with is that the MOB will not just be a physical marker but a genetic marker. It may even have beast or animal DNA. Now for the denials. Just a small bit of duckduckgoing will reveal that most sources are saying this therapy is not going to change your DNA permanently. Sadly, there have been no studies to this effect. However, we know it is possible because there is an enzyme in our bodies that actually writes RNA backward into our DNA (reverse transcriptase).

While they say that the mRNA just degrades, I have to ask, then how is it doing anything? What we do know is that this jab is overwriting our mRNA, which controls what our cells do.

Essentially, this mRNA is hijacking our cell's machinery to make it manufacture something unnatural. Why would we want a pathogen constantly being produced in our bodies, and what kind of harm can this do to certain tissues over the long haul.

Antibody Dependent Enhancement

Dr. Tom Cowan is another source who says based upon the total mortality figures of 2020 and their ability to actually isolate the Coronavirus, there is no reason to believe that there's any actual coronavirus out there. For my money, something doesn't add up. For example, there is no way they have met Koch's postulates (the standard for establishing the relationship between a microbe and a disease). And they are now saying they can't meet these requirements because Coronavirus is not a bacteria. I fail to see the logic. Meeting Koch's postulates would mean they have isolated the virus, introduced it to a new host causing a breakout infection, and then re-isolated the virus from the secondary host.

They have not been able to do this, which is why the PCR test is inaccurate. In fact, none of the vaccines have any attenuated (disabled) Covid virus inside of them. Dr. Simone Gold of americasfrontlinedoctors.com has talked about why this is the case. Dr. Gold says that when they tried inserting dead or attenuated Covid viruses in people, they encountered something called Antibody Dependent Enhancement or ADE. Essentially, when vaccinated subjects were later exposed to other naturally occurring strains of Covid, they showed a hyperimmune response that resulted in increased mortality. ADE is also described as a known hazard in an interview of Dr. J. Mercola's by Robert F. Kennedy Jr.

- https://forbiddenknowledgetv.net/dr-simone-gold-the-truth-about-the-cv19-vaccine/

- https://www.globalresearch.ca/well-known-hazards-coronavirus-vaccines/5712494

While we will cover more of this later, ADE would explain why they are messing with our RNA instead of going the traditional route. While virtually every site states that they have isolated this virus many times, why don't we have a better test than the PCR test? Here is the link to "Letters to the CDC and their Responses Concerning the Existence of SARS CoV-2 Renamed SARS CoV-19" that indicates some questions still exist about the isolation of CoV-19.

- https://www.drrobertyoung.com/post/letters-to-the-cdc-and-their-responses-concerning-the-existence-of-sars-cov-2-renamed-sars-cov-19?utm_campaign=ae94a173-16c b-4016-8c81-8e116deda716&utm_source=so&utm_ medium=mail&cid=8486780f-da1f-4521-b90f-6e16cd07da5c

- https://www.westonaprice.org/podcast/242-are-germs-the-enemy/

Not a Vaccine

According to the "Coronavirus Misinformation Tracking Center," neither US Centers for Disease Control and Prevention nor the US Food and Drug Administration stipulate that vaccines must both provide immunity and block transmission of a virus. However, that is certainly what traditional vaccines do. We could also say that if they don't do these things, then they don't work in the traditional sense either. The problem is that they are suddenly re-defining vaccines. In the fact checkers' rebuttal of Dr. Marten, they use CDC spokesperson Kristen Nordlund as their source. "There are many ways to define it, but the CDC describes a vaccine as a product that stimulates a person's immune system to produce immunity to a specific disease, protecting the person from that disease."

While they are saying mRNA vaccines meet this definition,

that is impossible because mRNA therapy does not produce specific immunity to Covid. People still have to wear masks and keep a social distance. Of course, you can argue that there is some lessening of symptoms but certainly not specific immunity. Either way, this does not meet the CDC's definition of a vaccine.

Even if they use the FDA's definition stating, "Vaccination stimulates the body's immune system to build up defenses against the infectious bacteria or virus (organism) without causing the disease." The problem is they are not (using a virus for) stimulating the immune system. They are hijacking the machinery of your cells using mRNA to force them to manufacture a spike protein, which causes a disease. Even Bill Gates admits that 80% of the people taking the jab get sick. So once again, this jab does not meet the definition of a vaccine because it actively makes us sick.

• https://www.youtube.com/watch?v=I68yBABRiQc

Unfortunately, we see the beginnings of a new experiment of a genetic nature carried out on the general public under an emergency order. With no long-term studies, how have they made people so afraid of catching Covid even if you are the right age and have no underlying conditions? Again, natural herd immunity is what 55,000 doctors are recommending as the best approach. If they both make us sick, then isn't the natural way the best choice?

The Cytokine Storm

Even though Facebook will not let me post this study, as it has been proven false from their perspective, Dr. Dolores Cahill, (Professor at the University of Dublin) makes some great arguments and cites proven research about the harmful, potential complications of mRNA vaccines. She also speaks about why it has been so difficult to get an actual Coronavirus vaccine, which we have previously mentioned as Antibody Dependent Enhancement. In one of the studies on Covid mRNA vaccines, mice exhibited a hypersensitivity upon future exposure to SARS-COV, which means they died in significant numbers. Their conclusion was "Caution in proceeding to application of a SARS-COV vaccine in humans is indicated."

- https://pubmed.ncbi.nlm.nih.gov/22536382/

The hypothesis is that when the mice were exposed to naturally occurring Covid, their bodies noticed that the same marker is present in each one of its own cells, and thus the immune system began attacking its own vital organs. This type of ADE creates a massive autoimmune response called "cytokines storm," which can lead to major organ failure and death. While the cytokines storm has been documented in some Covid cases around the globe, this idea has been hotly contested. Consequently, the only way we can refute this argument is time itself. As a final warning, Professor Dolores Cahill believes that people will start dying within eight months to just over a year after taking the first mRNA vaccines.

- https://www.bitchute.com/video/Dxjp6nkwhWn8/?fb-clid=IwAR306D7o8AvYskdYCZQCR2v5Bffj6o1-3XRSMxhkN968mkrdlAtUgsZRDOE

While they are saying the human military trials of mRNA went better than they did for the mice, no one can say there are any long-term studies on animals or humans. Corners have been cut, as no specific analysis has been done on the effects to our major organs, DNA, pregnant women, or fertility. There simply hasn't been enough time elapsed to be conclusive about the long-term effects of mRNA vaccines. Unfortunately, the Daily Expose is already saying there is evidence of Antibody Dependent Enhancement because the majority of Covid deaths are the fully vaccinated, and A&E attendance is breaking records. They are breaking records even after the vast majority have already taken the jab. Now let that sink in.

- https://dailyexpose.co.uk/2021/06/20/evidence-of-antibod-

y-dependent-enhancement-majority-of-covid-deaths-are-
the-fully-vaccinated-and-ae-attendance-is-breaking-
records/

On another note, both Professor Delores Cahill and Ole Damme believe experimental biological agents are being peddled as safe and effective "vaccines." Dr. Cahill also agrees that when we take this vaccine, we will now be a genetically modified human being because our bodies do not normally manufacture foreign substances. Essentially, we have to be genetically altered to manufacture something outside of what our DNA is encoded for.

- https://podcasts.apple.com/us/podcast/sgt-reports-the-pro-
  paganda-antidote/id1502568407?i=1000513523722

The issue then becomes whether this genetic modification is permanent, or whether it leaves some type of residual markers. Either way, I am not willing to take the chance. (Some vaccines may have self amplifying or saRNA, which removes the stop and start codon, making it permanent.)

Lastly, the following is another article by Dr. Lee Merritt, who references another animal study where the subjects died due to "antibody dependent enhancement" (ADE) after being injected with mRNA Technology.

- https://varjager.wordpress.com/2021/01/30/dr-lee-merritt-
  in-animal-studies-after-being-injected-with-mrna-tech-
  nology-all-animals-died-upon-reinfection/

A Crime Against Humanity

This hypersensitivity to Covid because of previous vaccinations was also something that the movie *Plandemic* (https://plan-demicvideo.com) alluded to. Yet, the real issue here is that I am not allowed to trust in God and what He did when He made my body. Trusting in God and the DNA that He wrote is simply not allowed, even though I have no personal risk of dying from Covid, and natural immunity works just fine. I must irrationally believe I am going to die even though the evidence says otherwise. The following is a good study showing that God's natural immunity is better than vaccines, along with one by the British Journal of Medicine admitting no vaccine is perfectly safe.

- https://iythealth.com/vaccines-weaken-immune-system/

- https://www.bmj.com/rapid-response/2011/10/30/how-can-vaccines-cause-damage

Vaccination in Israel:
Challenging mortality figures

According to IsraelNationsNews.com, there is a mismatch between the data published by the authorities and the reality on the ground. In January 2021, there were 40 times as many vaccine adverse events compared to other years; mortality is higher. Essentially, the authors say, "Vaccinations have caused more deaths than the coronavirus would have caused during the same period." And, "this is a new Holocaust," that is happening because they are not "able to communicate on this vital information" to their fellow citizens.

- https://www.israelnationalnews.com/News/News.aspx/ 297051?fbclid=IwAR1pydehEj1r_Udto1nVPBmjGxxpS0 u WX06GIfeR9zLwQ2cLv5W5XO8E9A

The Vaccine Isn't Safe

To date, all of the COVID-19 Vaccines specifically say that they are an "unapproved vaccine that may prevent COVID-19." There is no FDA-approved vaccine to prevent COVID-19. The FDA has authorized the emergency use of the COVID-19 vaccine to prevent COVID-19 in individuals 18 years of age and older under an Emergency Use Authorization (EUA). Even the new supposed FDA "full approval" of the Pfizer jab is a ruse. All it did was extend its emergency use for Pfizer and approved another product from BioNTech called Comirnaty, which isn't even on the market yet.

- https://journal-neo.org/2021/08/30/scandal-behind-the-fda-fake-approval-of-pfizer-jab/

The FDA refused to have an open hearing or include the statistics from VAERS, which is the Vaccine Adverse Events Reporting System. Tragically, VAERS is reporting over 14,923 adverse reports through July 30, 2021. Some of the adverse reactions included the following: 12,366 deaths, 46,036 hospitalizations, 68,040 urgent care visits, 92,527 office visits, 4,759 anaphylaxis, 4,044 Bell's palsy, 1,381 miscarriages, 5,236 heart attacks, 3,728 myocarditis/pericarditis, 14,251 permanently disabled, 12,104 life-threatening, and 23,354 severe reactions. This is especially disturbing since everyone is still telling pregnant women to get vaccinated, but, in this case, unborn children's lives don't matter. Yet, adverse reactions like these have even closed schools in Michigan, Ohio, and New York.

- https://www.openvaers.com/covid-data
- https://thevaccinereaction.org/2021/03/severe-reactions-to-covid-19-vaccine-close-schools-in-michigan-ohio-and-new-york/

Tucker Carlson helped put that into perspective when he showed that in just four months of taking the Covid jab, more people have been killed than from all the vaccines for the past 15.5 years.

- https://www.foxnews.com/opinion/tucker-carlson-how-many-americans-have-died-after-taking-the-covid-vaccine

Additionally, here is a great article by Dr. Sherri Tenpenny showing 20 different ways Covid jabs can injure or kill us.

- https://amigraineurslife.files.wordpress.com/2021/05/dr.-tenpenny-20-moi-list.pdf

Many people have also become aware that the CDC had to hold an emergency meeting over the alarming number of cases of heart inflammation in young vaccine recipients. Like Israel before them, the CDC Officials have had to admit there have been more hospitalizations of young people due to the Covid jab.

- https://www.breitbart.com/health/2021/06/14/cdc-holding-emergency-meeting-over-cases-of-heart-inflam-mation-disorder-young-coronavirus-vaccine-recipients/

- https://www.thegatewaypundit.com/2021/06/not-making-headlines-cdc-officials-admit-hospitalizations-young-people-vaccine-actual-covid-virus-including-huge-number-heart-problems-reported/

While most people will not listen to anyone that is not on TV, why is the world not listening to the inventor of the mRNA vaccine? On the June 29, 2021 episode of "The Highwire, with Del Bigtree," he interviews Dr. Robert Malone, one of the inventors of mRNA. Dr. Malone details his concerns that he reported to the FDA in September 2020 in an effort to get them to stop the vaccine from moving forward. He specifically reports that spike proteins are capable of opening the blood brain barrier, how the lipids envelopes containing the mRNA accumulate in the ovaries, and how the vaccine is dangerous for children.

- https://podcasts.apple.com/us/podcast/the-highwire-with-del-bigtree/id1227863378?i=1000527254204

While it is hard to get doctors to go on record, two other brave doctors, Dr. Wolfgang Wodarg and Dr. Michael Yeadon, have issued a motion for administrative and regulatory action to the European Medicines Agency (EMA) regarding the new mRNA coronavirus vaccines developed by Pfizer/BioNTech. They warn that the vaccines can attack placenta cells, causing infertility.

- https://rightsfreedoms.wordpress.com/2021/04/20/new-mrna-vaccine-could-cause-immune-cells-to-attack-placenta-cells-causing-female-infertility-miscarriage-or-birth-defects/

- https://childrenshealthdefense.org/defender/mrna-technology-covid-vaccine-lipid-nanoparticles-accumulate-ovaries/

Dr. Michael Yeadon is especially noteworthy because he is the former Vice President of Pfizer and an Allergy & Respiratory Therapeutic Area expert with 23 years in the pharmaceutical industry. He trained as a biochemist and pharmacologist, obtaining his PhD from the University of Surrey in 1988. But here is an interview with him that is clearly sounding an alarm to all of us.

- https://podcasts.apple.com/us/podcast/former-pfizer-vice-president-dr-mike-yeadon-speaks-out/id1552000243?i=1000522111591

Another curiosity of the Covid jab is that most vaccines seem to stay in the arm, but here is a postmortem study of a patient where viral RNA is found in every organ of the body, which means these genetic codes are passing the blood brain barrier. They may also be causing blood clots and destroying brain cells.

- https://halturnerradioshow.com/index.php/en/news-page/world/global-time-bomb-first-case-of-postmortem-study-of-patient-vaccinated-against-sars-cov-2-mrna-found-in-every-organ-of-the-body

- https://thebl.tv/us-news/study-shows-covid-19-mrna-based-vaccines-may-destroy-brain-cells.html

- https://thetruedefender.com/its-official-a-clear-link-between-astrazeneca-and-blood-clots-in-the-human-brain-is-confirmed/

Dr. Ryan Cole MD also gives a clarification of what these injections can potentially do in the head and other organs of the vaccinated people.

- https://rumble.com/vkopys-a-pathologist-summary-of-what-these-jabs-do-to-the-brain-and-other-organs.html

Another voice, Dr. Geert Vanden Bossche, PhD, DVM is an internationally recognized expert on vaccines and had even directed vaccine production for the Bill and Melinda Gates Foundation. Geert is alarmed at the vaccination enforcement and lockdowns. He believes "immune escape" (not allowing ourselves to be exposed to naturally occurring antigens) will suppress our "innate immunity" and achieve the opposite of herd immunity. Dr. Geert also believes "acquired immunity" from vaccines could result in vaccine-resistant variants of the virus or super viruses. If correct, this predicts much larger and more destructive pandemics in the future. Essentially, mass vaccinations during a pandemic are contra-indicated. Geert's dire warning—"We are at the eve of a huge disaster."

This idea of creating variants due to over-vaccination with even worse outcomes is also echoed by Nobel Prize winner Professor Luc Montagnier, when he said, "It's the vaccination that's creating the variants." Everyone knows that viruses are changing and mutating, and most epidemiologists are aware that Antibody-Dependent Enhancement can threaten the whole world with worse outbreaks!

- https://thetruedefender.com/breaking-nobel-prize-winner-exposes-that-covid-shots-create-variants/

Additionally, here is a study written by Dr. J. Bart Classen,

MD, indicating that COVID-19 jabs can represent a cure worse than the disease. In this case, we are talking about prion disease, which is more commonly called Mad Cow Disease.

- https://dundasvalley.files.wordpress.com/2021/03/covid19-rna-based-vaccines-and-the-risk-of-prion-disease-1503.pdf

Along these same lines, Dr. Dan Shock, a functional family medicine physician specially trained in immunology and inflammation regulation, addressed many of these same concerns to the Mt Vernon School Board. Dr. Shock dared to defy what the CDC and the NIH are recommending for schools—masks and vaccines. Whether you agree with him or not, there is something seriously wrong with the vaccine's effectiveness, and why a new variant is out so soon, and in the summer, no less. Here is what he said:

> We are 18 months into this, and we are still having a problem, and the reason is because we are doing things that are not useful... There is no cure for Covid any more than there is a cure for the common cold... Why is a vaccine having a breakout in the middle of the summer when respiratory viruses don't do that??? And to help you understand that, you need to know the condition is called antibody mediated viral enhancement (essentially ADE) That is a condition done when vaccines work wrong, as they did in every coronavirus study done with animals... (The Vaccine) causes our immune system to fight the virus wrong and let the virus become worse than it would have been with a native infection, and that is why you were seeing an outbreak right now.

- https://www.youtube.com/watch?v=LLYBqjX0l0g

Informed Consent

As we have said previously, the emergency order (EUA) is what allows everyone to ignore the safeguards of the healthcare system and practice what would normally be called malpractice. Even though these vaccines specifically say that they are an "unapproved vaccine that may prevent COVID-19," they do not require informed consent to be given or signed. Their refusal to disclose any pertinent medical facts surrounding the complications represents fraud at the highest level and breaks the freedom of information act. I am simply astonished that anyone over twelve can verbally consent to take the vaccine, despite no disclosure of the potential side effects.

To help us all understand just how ridiculous all of this is, just watch any commercial on TV about any drug they are advertising. Most of the commercial is spent notifying the potential customers of the negative side effects of the medication. With all these protective measures gone, who is going to protect us? It gets worse. In stunning fashion, the CDC no longer keeps track of complications from the supposed vaccines. Health care providers and consumers optionally report events to the VAERS system, which is why it is believed that only 1-10% of the complications have been reported.

Still, I keep asking myself, where is the emergency? We have blatantly disregarded the normal safeguards that have kept the unthinkable from happening. Again, this is like being told we have to run into four lanes of traffic just to save a $3 ball. Indeed, the cure is worse than the disease. Breaking any of these normal procedures is grounds for malpractice, and they are breaking them all. Yet, none of this farce would be happening if Congress had not completely taken away all liability surrounding the Covid narrative. Meanwhile, everyone knows when we do things in a rush, bad things can happen.

- https://www.msn.com/en-us/health/medical/cdc-limits-

review-of-vaccinated-but-infected-draws-concern/ar-
BB1gx1au

Recombinant DNA

Regarding the mRNA in this supposed vaccine, the official stance is that these codes dissipate, but evidence still surfaces that these genetic codes are moving throughout the body. Unfortunately, there is no way to remove them once the jab has been given. What is also novel is that they seem to need multiple booster shots. Curiously, this type of therapy is similar to something called recombinant DNA therapy or rDNA. Recombinant DNA therapy is a corrective form of gene therapy for those suffering from genetic birth defects, but it is interesting that they also use mRNA.

In the case of recombinant DNA therapy, they take two pieces of DNA or RNA and recombine them to make new DNA. Changing our DNA is not just the goal for helping people with birth defects, it is also the goal of the super-soldier program. It's hard to say how successful they have been, but we know they need multiple jabs over a long period of time. What is also worrisome is that the Covid narrative gives them this kind of access to our bodies. With the new magnetic therapies and the development of CRISPR technology, they can rapidly sequence genetic material into anything they like. Because of these breakthroughs and similarities to other genetic therapies, the effect of the Covid jab on our DNA comes into question.

• https://www.ncbi.nlm.nih.gov/pmc/articles/PMC5178364/

Vaccine Boosters

On a podcast, former Pfizer Vice President, Dr. Mike Yeadon, spoke to Robert F. Kennedy Jr. about the unlikelihood that the Covid vaccine boosters being pushed are actually boosters. Dr. Yeadon mentioned that they might tie into something far more nefarious than we might have suspected. As we will see, some of the available technologies can assemble themselves, which is why the true agenda may not be accomplished all in one shot. They may need multiple access points. But once we understand the kind of available technology, it is very disturbing that there is no full disclosure as to the vaccine's proprietary ingredients.

- https://factcheckvaccine.com/2021/05/former-pfizer-vice-president-dr-mike-yeadon-speaks-out-on-rfk-jr-the-defender-podcast-may-7-2021/

Dr. Robert Malone, the inventor of mRNA technology, has certainly questioned the rationale for mandatory jabs but doesn't address boosters specifically. However, Dr. Malone does cite four flawed assumptions in Biden's Covid strategy. "The first is that universal vaccination can eradicate the virus and secure economic recovery by achieving herd immunity throughout the country. The second assumption is that the vaccines are (near) perfectly effective. However, our currently available vaccines are quite "leaky." The third assumption is that the vaccines are safe. The failure of the fourth "durability" assumption is the most alarming and perplexing. It now appears our current vaccines are likely to offer a mere 180-day window of protection—a decided lack of durability underscored by scientific evidence from Israel and confirmed by Pfizer, the Department of Health and Human Services, and other countries."

Notice that this affirms much of what we have been reporting so far. But one of the finer points of the interview also brought up a very real danger of the vaccine arms race: over-vaccinating populations (just like over using antibiotics) is likely to produce "super strains" of the virus. "The more people you vaccinate, the greater the number of vaccine-resistant mutations you are likely to get, the less durable the vaccines will become, ever more powerful vaccines will have to be developed, and individuals will be exposed to more and more risk."

• https://www.washingtontimes.com/news/2021/aug/5/
biden-teams-misguided-and-deadly-covid-19-vaccine-/

The media is certainly reporting solely on the new Delta strain.
Many sources are saying the unvaccinated are to blame. But if their
jab worked, then how are the unvaccinated to blame? It is commonly known that the overuse of antibiotics has produced super
strains of bacteria. Why wouldn't viruses work the same? Dr.
Malone specifically refutes the idea that somehow the unvaccinated
have caused new stains or the failure of the jabs. In fact, it is the
other way around. Over-vaccinating is likely to produce super
strains of the virus, which is what Dr. Geert Vanden Bossche has
previously said.

Now that the CDC has approved said vaccine booster, they
may as well have admitted that the supposed vaccine didn't work.
Indeed, the CDC director, Rochelle Walensky, did admit that the
supposed vaccine didn't stop the presence of Covid or someone's
ability to be spread Covid, which is why everyone is back to
masking up and social distancing. Even Dr. Fauci admitted that
the Delta variant is as contagious as the chickenpox, even by fully
vaccinated people.

So, why was Dr. Fauci alarmed? "The fact that you have a high
level of virus in the nasal pharynx of an infected person who has a
breakthrough (of symptoms), namely was vaccinated… (and) is
now capable of transmitting that infection to an uninfected
person." Yes, that should be alarming because it means the vaccine
doesn't work. More importantly, they stopped keeping statistics on
the vaccinated, and they released them with no restrictions, which
means they made this whole thing worse.

While "three mask" Tony maintains that the vaccine doesn't
work because "we are dealing with a different virus," his solution is
to just "get as many people vaccinated as we possibly can," even
though the vaccinated are showing up at the hospital like everyone
else. Furthermore, his argument about how most of the people who

die of Covid are the unvaccinated doesn't hold water because the vaccine hasn't been around long enough, and conveniently, they didn't keep track of the vaccinated.

By this point, it is now clear that the vaccinated are catching it, spreading it, and going to the hospitals just like the rest of us. But the argument to take the vaccine, just like the emergency order, falls like a deck of cards if we have no risk of dying. It is statistics like these that are why americasfrontlineocors.com has said the only people who should consider taking this jab is if they are over 65 or have 2.3 comorbidities. Again, if we are not at risk of dying, then why would we do anything differently? Why would we take an experimental jab, close everything, stay home, and lose everything we have for virtually no risk?

- https://www.npr.org/2021/07/30/1022909501/dr-anthony-fauci-talks-about-alarming-new-data-on-breakthrough-infections

- (Previously listed) https://www.cnbc.com/2021/07/30/cdc-study-shows-74percent-of-people-infected-in-massachu-setts-covid-outbreak-were-fully-vaccinated.html?__source=sharebar%7Cfacebook&par=sharebar&fbclid=IwAR3Nzc kpIZlV9CtWeCjlN1SlsGOVUaPWQ1cXLXCnb52rGX KIwNNUAeHTRpk

Shockingly, none of this changes their recommendations on the jab? Nope, full steam ahead. Still not getting it? Neither am I. But the official line on the boosters is summarized quite well by Dr. David Bauer. Dr. Bauer heads up the RNA virus replication laboratory at the Francis Crick Institute, and here is what he had to say about both Covid immunity and vaccination:

So, the key message from our findings is that we found that recipients of the Pfizer vaccine, those who have 2 doses, have about 5- to 6-fold lower amounts of neutralizing antibodies. These are sort of gold standard anti-bodies, which block the viruses from getting into your cells in the first place. So, we found that is less with people with two doses ... we also found that for people with one dose they are less likely to have these antibodies in their blood. Perhaps most importantly, for all of us going forward, the older you are, the lower your levels are likely to be, and the times since you have had your second jab, the lower your levels are also likely to be. So, that is telling us that we will need to prioritize boosters for older and more vulnerable coming up soon especially if this new variant spreads.

- https://www.msn.com/en-gb/news/other/dr-david-bauer-pfizer-vaccine-produces-fewer-key-antibodies/vi-AAKHPO1

So, let me get this straight. This vaccine lowers my "gold standard" antibodies by 5-6 times, and your solution is just to take another one? But that is what he says. Not only is this whole repeated jab scenario starting to look like genetic therapy, but it is also starting to look like the very definition of a good drug because you have to take it for a lifetime. The bad news is the obvious reason they have approved another booster is because people could die without it, and their current jab is the reason. Could this be because they have lowered the levels of the most desirable neutralizing antibodies?

Naturally, one would think that lower antibodies would lead to a lower level of our immune response and higher deaths. Unfortunately, these lowered levels of antibodies sounds eerily similar to the Antibody Dependent Enhancement (ADE) syndrome we have already talked about. Dr. Malone also echoes this concern after a report came out by Jason D. Meister saying, "Vaccinated individuals could have higher levels of virus and infect others amid the surge of cases driven by the Delta variant." While Dr. Fauci maintains nasal titers are similar for vaccinated to the unvaccinated, Dr. Malone believes the blood titers are considerably more accurate than the nasal version. If this report is true, then Dr. Malone believes this could be a smoking gun for ADE.

- https://z3news.com/w/dr-robert-malone-inventor-of-mrna-technology-signals-the-worst-case-scenario-about-covid-19-vaccines/

- https://luis46pr.wordpress.com/2021/07/29/usa-today-deletes-nbc-news-report-showing-covid-vaccinated-spread-virus/

On his show, *The Highwire*, Del Bigtree illustrates how "neutralizing" antibodies produce a more general immunity. Consequently, neutralizing antibodies are better than specific immunity because they can intercept all variants, not just a specific variant. His illustration works just like a diagram of X's and O's for football. Notice that the variant viruses are lined up on the left. Their goal is to penetrate the body's defenses. The X represents a particular kind of virus paired to a particular antibody. In the first illustration, the X's can only intercept X's, which leaves M, L, and P to penetrate the body. But with general immunity, the O's can intercept any of the variants, which leaves us better protected.

Specific Immunity			**General Immunity**		
Virus		Vax Antibodies	Virus		Natural Antibodies
A	←	A	A	←	O
B	→	A	B	←	O
C	→	A	C	←	O
D	→	A	D	←	O

So, here is what I have gleaned so far. Not only does the jab not provide immunity, but it also lowers our neutralizing antibodies, which could cause significant health complications for the vaccinated in the near future. To top it off, the overuse of vaccines during a pandemic could lead to the creation of viral super strains. Lowered immunity, combined with viral super strains, does not sound like a good combination. Could this be why the history of actual Covid containing vaccines has included the occurrence of ADE? Is anyone getting goosebumps yet? Does it really sound far-fetched that we are in danger of actually creating an even bigger pandemic?

But before I ever knew any of this, the following points are why I didn't take the jab. First, humanity is here today because we have survived based upon our natural God-given immunity. Second, why would I trust a scientist who was rushed to beat his competition to re-write my God-given mRNA codes? This jab will stop my body from making the proteins it needs, and instead, man-ufacture a pathogenic spike protein. Indeed, we have no long-term testing on humans or animals. The last reason why I didn't take the jab is that my Bible has been telling me to be looking for a "cause" to come into the world surrounded by deception and characterized by an insatiable need to get access to my body. Is it a coincidence that they want access to my temple? I think not.

The Cabal of Death

If the Covid narrative is not real, with respect to being statisti-cally different, then we have a huge problem. Something is trying to take control of the entire world. It is powerful, organized, and coordinated beyond what most of us can imagine. This entity is something we will spend quite a bit of time on in chapter eight, but for now we will call it "Mystery Babylon." However, since this madness has begun, we have seen many of the players who are in-volved—whole countries, governments, agencies, politicians, the entire media, every internet search engine, labs, scientists, the WHO, video platforms, and virtually all social media.

Just since the US elections of 2020, we have seen Apple,

Google, Amazon, Twitter, Facebook, Ford, GM, and many others begin boycotts and outright censorship of conservative voices and even a sitting president. Unfortunately, just a few groups of people own our media, and the bias is palpable on virtually every piece of news. Even the US Federal Reserve (owner of our national debt) is not owned by the government. Essentially, they are mostly the same people who own the IMF or International Monetary Fund. These international bankers, merchants, and dignitaries are the people who really run the world, and some of them aren't even part of the 62 people we have already mentioned.

Agenda 21 and ID2020 are two initiatives that also tap into some of the endgames that the world's elite have planned for us. Dr. Carrie Madej is a doctor who has spoken out on multiple platforms about how the true ingredients of these supposed vaccines have not been revealed. She also maintains that there has been no independent analysis of any of them. Based upon some of the beastly technologies currently available, Dr. Madej details how nanotechnologies offer a frightening amount of control for all those who take them. Nanotechnologies alone are what make these supposed vaccines different than anything before them.

Dr. Carrie Madej also talks about how something is going on with fertility in women even though they are unvaccinated, and she proposes a few possibilities. One of them is shedding, which is clearly talked about in some of the vaccine companies own research, but they never disclose this to the public because they have no liability. What is shocking is that some nanotechnologies have the ability to know everything you do and then upload all of that to the Internet. Dr. Madej also shares how the vaccine companies knew that the vaccines still allowed for infection and transmission, but again, they had no liability.

Pfizer's documents admit Covid vaccines will shed infectious particles to others.

"An occupational exposure occurs when a person receives unplanned direct contact with a vaccine test subject, which may or may not lead to the occurrence of an adverse event," the Pfizer document warns. "These people may include health care providers, family members, and other people who are around the trial participant."

- https://afinalwarning.com/515889.html

- https://christiansfortruth.com/confirmed-covid-vacci-nated-people-can-shed-spike-proteins-and-harm-the-un-vaccinated/

Probably the most troubling thing Dr. Madej shares is how RNA can retro-integrate into our DNA because we have an enzyme that allows for that to happen. She also references a supreme court justice ruling that allows someone to patent a human being if the person carries the manufacturer's unique genetic code. All this information has explosive implications, and especially as we expose some of these ingredients and what they do. Certainly, Dr. Madej will not be the only one with these same talking points. It is also hard to miss the idea that infertility would certainly accomplish the depopulation goals of Agenda 21.

- https://www.brighteon.com/9933e3e9-790b-4c8b-a65a-2ebf81c97f99

Deathly Ingredients

It is difficult to examine the ingredients of these supposed vaccines. One of the ingredients listed for Moderna, which is backed by Bill Gates, is SM-102, which is linked to cancer, infertility, and death. The article below states that this ingredient is, "For research use only, not for human or veterinary use… The safety data sheet also lists cancer, infertility, kidney, liver, and central nervous system damage as possible health hazards … The vaccine ingredient is said to be 'Fatal in contact with skin,' and 'Toxic to aquatic life with long lasting effects.'" Can we also call these supposed vaccines poison?

- https://www.infowars.com/posts/horrifying-bombshell-connecticut-warns-moderna-vax-contains-deadly-poison/

Dr. Vladimir Zelenko has treated some of the most famous people in the world. He also testified about the ingredients of the vaccine before the Israeli Rabbinical court. Dr. Zelenko called it a "poison death shot." His testimony is one of the most riveting that I have seen. Then Dr. Zelenko explains his rationale for any treatment, "Is it safe, does it work, and is it necessary?" Here is some of what I heard him say regarding each of these issues. Why would we give someone experimental treatments when they have no risk of dying? Israel is over 80% vaccinated. Why take a third shot that didn't work the first two times?

When it comes to the safety of the jab, Dr. Zelenko mentions blood clots, myocarditis, infertility, decreased sperm count, cancer, and autoimmune conditions. He also mentions an article in the *New England Journal of Medicine* that found the risk of miscarriage went up from 10% to 80%. Dr. Zelenko also agrees there is a strong risk for Pathogenic Priming or ADE. Dr. Zelenko also affirms that children do not need any treatment for Covid, but fear is causing us to sacrifice our children. Like Dr. McCullough, Dr. Zelenko says if we can treat people with Covid with the right timing, we can prevent 85% of the deaths.

Probably the most powerful thing he says is how he is threatened daily and how he is risking his family, career, and safety in order to tell us what he is telling us. He goes on to say, natural immunity is superior to the vaccination, so "Why would I take a poison death shot?" What he says next is prophetic because Dr. Zelenko testifies to the Rabbinical Priesthood that they are worshipping a false god. He asks them if they are going to bow down to God or to man.

- https://americasfrontlinedoctors.org/frontlinenews/poison-death-shot-dr-zelenko-testifies-before-israeli-rabbinical-court/

Lastly, Dr. Zelenko quotes Nobel Laureate Luc Montagnier as saying, "We're in unknown territory and proclaim mandatory vaccines for everyone? It's insanity. It's vaccination insanity that I absolutely condemn... This is the biggest risk to humanity and the biggest risk of genocide in the history of humanity."

- https://rairfoundation.com/nobel-laureate-luc-montagnier-warns-covid-vaccine-may-lead-to-neurodegenerative-illness-video/

Beast Technology

While we have been focusing on vaccines, there are many other technologies that fit the connotations of the MOB scenario. One of the most striking is something called "luciferase," and it can be delivered through a micro-needling patch or quantum dot tattoo. This nanotechnology is named after Lucifer because it gives off light once it's activated with a scanner.

- https://stillnessinthestorm.com/2020/09/must-read-an-enzyme-called-luciferase-is-what-makes-bill-gates-implantable-vaccine-work-vaccine-id/

Dr. Joseph Mercola calls this a Rockefeller tracking plan. He also notes how Bill Gates has gone on record saying, "Life will not go back to normal until we have the ability to vaccinate the entire global population against COVID-19." The only way to verify this solution would be a vaccine tracking system embedded in our bodies, but that is just the tip of the iceberg of what they can do. My question to the skeptics is, "If there is never to be hidden technology in vaccines, then why are most genetic therapies and biometrics tracking devices specifically designed to be used with vaccines? More specifically, why did documents from Moderna call the vaccine an operating system, and can this be our first step towards transhumanism?

- https://fort-russ.com/2020/05/dr-mercola-horrifying-id2020-quantum-dot-tattoo-bill-gates-and-rockefeller-tracking-plan/

- https://principia-scientific.com/modernas-covid-injection-is-an-operating-system-is-this-transhumanism/

What is disturbing about Luciferase is not just the name or the 060606 ending to the patent number, it is that Luciferase allows them to brand us with an invisible marker that tells them everything about us. Remember, we have already been told by the ID2020 agenda that each person will eventually be branded with a unique identifier like any other product ID. This kind of mark would likely be the end of the cash system, as well as the end of our independence.

But the scariest tech out there is DARPA's Hydrogel, which places nanobots inside our bodies. They would have the ability to assemble, dis-assemble, gather personal information, and communicate through the cloud to an artificial intelligence. Not only would they know everything about us, but they may be able to execute commands, deliver medications, and possibly manipulate our DNA. Unfortunately, DARPA also partners with Profusa, whose main goal is "pioneering tissue-integrating biosensors for continuous monitoring of body chemistries." Their website explains how it works.

- https://z3news.com/w/darpa-injectable-solution-enables-government-tracking-monitoring-recipients/

Changing Our DNA

While many of us may still be struggling with the idea that

this supposed vaccine is genetic therapy, page 70 of Moderna's Quarterly Report affirms that RNA codes are being changed from what they were. But some might immediately say, "Yes, but this jab doesn't change our DNA." There are two issues. First, RNA controls our cells' actions, while DNA carries the words or information of what we are supposed to do. Remembering that "actions speak louder than words" helps us understand just how important RNA really is. The second part is that RNA can also write backwards to DNA, but is that happening with this jab?

Bombshell: Moderna Chief Medical Officer Admits MRNA Alters DNA

- https://thewashingtonstandard.com/bombshell-moderna-chief-medical-officer-admits-mrna-alters-dna/

- https://www.sec.gov/Archives/edgar/data/1682852/000168285220000017/mrna-20200630.htm

Not only does Tal Zaks, chief medical officer of Moderna, say that this vaccine alters or recodes our RNA, but he affirms that it also alters our DNA permanently by "hacking the software of life." Here is what he means when he says that:

- When "changing" a line of code or "introducing" a line of code (referring to DNA), the "code" or DNA is then altered, meaning the individual or "subject" has now had their genome changed to what the "scientists" have coded. **The individual or subject is no longer a creation of God but a creation of man, meaning the individual or subject could be the object of a "patent."**

What did he just say? Did he just say that this vaccine alters our DNA? While our old DNA was obviously written by God, our new DNA is now written by men. Because we have been altered by man, like any other invention, we could be the subject of "patents," which is a title of ownership. A patent also implies a relationship between a creator with their creation. Companies like Monsanto have already obtained patents like this. For example, all they do is take the corn that God created, change some of the genetic codes, and then they can get a patent of ownership.

These rights of ownership are so strong that if one of Monsanto's seeds blows onto your land, you still must pay them their portion. What Mr. Zaks is referring to is that each person who takes the jab now has Moderna's codes, and that certainly could allow them to push for a patent. According to Dr. Madej, the Supreme Court has already ruled that it is possible to own another human being. But the question is whether this argument will hold up in the court of heaven. The idea of no longer being a creation of God should sound the alarm for every Christian. For myself, scarier words have never been spoken, which is why I will not allow anyone to change my genetic material.

The Subject of a Patent

Now, for the record, I am not 100% sure that these vaccines are altering the DNA in our chromosomes, but I am way more than 50% convinced. However, these new lines of thinking make it seem possible that we could reach a point where it is true with enough changes made. We really could be a new species. What we can say for sure is that some of our genetic codes of RNA are being over-written with a new man-made code, and that alone is a no-go for me.

It is a fact that this vaccine is changing our God-given mRNA to force our cells to produce what they want. However, I do not buy into Tal Zaks' argument completely that changing one line of coding in our RNA or DNA will cause us to stop being a creation of God. In the same way that putting aftermarket wheels on our new Ford does not stop it from being a Ford, I believe this is true of God and us. Consequently, we cannot fully conclude that these vaccines cause us to lose our salvation based upon this simple change alone. But clearly there is a point where every manufacturer no longer recognizes a car or truck as still being theirs because it has been so heavily modified.

While I do not know what the tipping point is where we are "no longer a creation of God," I do believe that a tipping point exists. I have used these genetic arguments of transhumanism for over 12 years now to help explain the mystery surrounding the MOB. The passing on of genetic markers alone represents why I believe these vaccines are the precursor to the MOB. However, when they won't tell us what is in them, there is technology available right now that could make this the real MOB if they were to sneak it in.

Another way manufacturers stand behind their creations is the idea of a warranty. But all warranties are voided if certain kinds of aftermarket upgrades are made, such as adding a supercharger or turbo charger. The issue of warranty may be the illustration that is the most compelling. Why do I say that? In life, Jesus is our warranty from God. As we will see, in Genesis 3, God promised that the seed (offspring) of the woman (Jesus) would one day win the battle over the seed of Satan. Therefore, we do not want to do anything that changes our seed or voids our connection with the One who gives us a warranty for redemption. Essentially, our seed or genetic material is part of what gives Jesus rights to us because He is related to us.

Remember, "It is impossible for the blood of bulls and goats to take away sins" (Hebrews 10:4). Jesus had to be born a man, die like a man, and be resurrected as a man to redeem mankind, which is why changing our genetic material could be the world's most dangerous idea. The last thing I will say is that it would be a mistake to think that this vaccine is doing nothing because this jab cannot be taken back. These genetic changes are likely to be passed on to all future generations. Humanity will never be the same.

Here are a few more studies to this effect. The first one is by Dr. Carrie Madej, who is part of America's Frontline Doctors.

• https://www.cnbsnews.live/documentaries/dr-carrie-madej-the-gene-code-injection-an-experiment-on-humanity/

• https://www.naturalnews.com/2021-04-09-april-9th-mrna-vaccines-may-edit-your-genes-through-retro-integration-dna-damage.html

• lbry.tv/@OYENEWS:e1/mrna-modify-dna:2

• https://phys.org/news/2020-01-rna-effect-dna.html

• https://childrenshealthdefense.org/defender/science-mrna-vaccines-alter-dna/

• https://proippatent.com/Infocenter/detail/47/what-is-patent-060606-microchip-and-famous-bill-gates-patent-number?lang=en

The World's Most Dangerous Agenda

By now some of you are starting to think that I have either lost my mind or I'm grasping at straws. However, I am not alone in my concerns over genetic changes that are being made to the human race. The best way to illustrate this concern would be to ask a question that was first asked back in 2004. "What is the world's most dangerous idea?" According to Francis Fukuyama, a Nobel peace prize-winning scientist, it is changing our DNA.

• https://www.au.dk/fukuyama/boger/essay/

Why? Changing our DNA would irreparably change who we are. Even more unfortunate, changing the DNA of a few people would change the DNA of the entire human race within four to five generations. At that point, none of the people that God created would be left. These genetic changes are yet another reason why we are seeing a convergence of modern technology and Bible prophecy that is getting harder to ignore. Consequently, we must further explore just what the implications of transhumanism are and why it is "the world's most dangerous idea."

But understanding just how important our DNA is to maintain our humanity is difficult to fathom. Consequently, of all the freedoms that have been lost since 2020, the rights to our bodies could be the greatest one of them all. More importantly, if a totalitarian government used any of the beastly technology that is currently available, we would all just be fish in the barrel. The other problem is that any of the freedoms we give to our government are never given back. So, tread carefully because we cannot give up the hallowed ground on which we walk.

5

Genetic Manipulation in the Bible

An Obsession with "Super"

In this chapter, we want to explore genetic narratives of the Bible and whether it has predicted this coming genetic revolution. More specifically, did the Bible predict that something like transhumanism would come along to offer something that Satan has been promising mankind since the Garden of Eden? It is becoming more obvious that our society is becoming obsessed with superheroes or people with superpowers. If we add in aliens, magic, and sorcery, we have the plot of virtually every new movie.

Yet, with all of this talk of superheroes, I want to remind us that Jesus is still the greatest superhero of all. Why? Because Jesus had to be born a man to redeem all of mankind. Someone who wasn't a man, with different DNA than ours, could not have achieved this superhuman feat because he wasn't fully human (Hebrews 10:4). This is the power of the Gospel, that through Christ, we will get a new body, destiny, identity, home, and power that are all more than super. The desire for this something more is buried so deep within our hearts because it is what we were created for.

Satan knows all too well how tempting this is for us because he is consumed by it himself. Consequently, the motivation to take the MOB may be more than just fear. It could simply be linked to our desire to be like God. Isn't that why we are so fascinated with both superheroes and the supernatural world? Wasn't this temptation to be super part of Satan's first spiel? Maybe it wasn't all fluff. Maybe the MOB will in some way fulfill part of Satan's promise to turn us into gods.

Altered Perception

What are some of the consequences of changing our DNA? Unfortunately, they could be endless. I have heard Dr. Tom Horn talk many times about how when we transfer quail DNA into chickens, they move their heads like quail and sound like quail. These are complex memories and patterns of behavior that are instantaneously changed. Applying this to human beings could turn them into something that is not fully human. Even Francis Fukuyama went on to write about "Our Posthuman Future: Consequences of the Biotechnology Revolution," and it wasn't good.

Looking at the super-soldier program may be our best illustration of what is possible. What exactly are they looking to change about humans in this program? Some of the scary truth comes out in the article, "DARPA Continues Human Experiments to Create Military Super Soldiers." In the article, DARPA specifically says they are trying to: "enhance a soldier's ability to kill without care or remorse, shows no fear, can fight battle after battle without fatigue, and generally behave more like a machine than a man."

Unfortunately, they have been experimenting on human beings in this way for more than 40 years. But who would call the soldier they are describing human? More importantly, who would want to sign up for that? Honestly, that description could easily be a description of your average demon. If you are still struggling with understanding how unlocking and sequencing DNA is changing mankind, then here are some movies to watch that might help to get a handle on just what is possible. Some regular movies with the same implications: *Transcendence, Avatar, Robocop, Ghost in a Shell, Spice,* and *Ex-Machina.* Listed below are two documentaries that deal with the subject.

- *INHUMAN: THE NEXT AND FINAL PHASE OF MANKIND IS HERE!*

- *Human Nature* and *Unnatural Selection* on Netflix - Detailing CRISPR technology

Transhumanism?

Originally transhumanism was changing our DNA and combining it with other species. Still, with the invention of CRISPR technology, it is possible to sequence our own designer DNA instead of splicing. People fail to understand that the fundamental tenet of transhumanism is to re-make mankind into a new image, and one of our own (or someone else's) choosing. We have the technology to combine species and make hybrids that are stronger, smarter, and live much longer. This is the supposedly positive side of altering our DNA, but in the process, we lose our humanity.

Nonetheless, if the promises of transhumanism come true, which is to make a better man than God did, then how might this also be another kind of cause that motivates the whole world to take this beastly marker? Who doesn't want to look better, live longer, and have superpowers? Unfortunately, no matter what your narrative is, changing our DNA would be the extinction of the human race, at least the one God created. God simply cannot say that He created us with the kinds of changes that are being proposed. This is the point where we would stop being what God created and become something else if we choose.

Essentially, this is the end of the human race and the beginning of another race. After all, from an evolutionary perspective, we are just evolving into gods. Wanting to be God is one of the distinguishing characteristic of Satan and his offspring. Certainly, the MOB would have to be considered the single most dangerous threat to salvation. Consequently, genetic manipulation of the human genome is the game-changer that the church is completely unaware of.

119

However, where their plan converges with the Bible is that they need access to our bodies to execute their plan. As we speak, our freedoms are under relentless assault. Wouldn't now be the perfect time to slip the world's most dangerous agenda into play? It could be argued that taking a vaccine is the main push of the COVID-19 deception. This elimination of the original genome could easily be the reason why God tells us that He has to return. Otherwise no one would be left (Matthew 24:22).

Maybe God is talking about His children—the ones who have His DNA, and the ones who still bear His image. But none of this is possible unless they get access to our bodies. Right now, they are making us comfortable with their pandemic model and things like DNA and RNA. But the question is: Did the Bible give us some huge hints that there might be a genetic component to the MOB?

For now, we need to understand that the coming of transhumanism asks a question that has been raging in mankind's mind since the temptation in the Garden of Eden: Do we want to be God's children, or do we want to be something of our own making? Do we want a relationship with God or do we want to be god? We must look deep within ourselves and decide what we want to be. We also have to remember that Satan's agenda has always been to have offspring that look like him.

From my perspective, this cannot be a coincidence that these are the first vaccines to have genetic components. However, based upon the available technologies and the vague descriptions of the supposed vaccines, we should all be moving with extreme caution. Indeed, there is too much at stake. So, my advice is to trust God and don't change anything God made.

The Precursor to MOB

While the first rocket didn't put a man on the moon, it did get off the ground. Likewise, it would be a mistake to think that changing our RNA is harmless. More importantly, we could be looking for a treatment plan instead of a "one and done" deal. However, rolling things out in stages would certainly avoid the obvious objections to the undeniable change that the MOB seems to cause. A better way to roll this out is to introduce something that comes in pieces, which the booster narrative provides. Essentially, the idea is we can't put a space station into orbit, but we can put the pieces up there.

Smaller changes could eventually produce behavioral or spiritual changes that somehow affect our conscience and relationship with God. What is obvious is that creatures with different DNA can see things we can't see. What am I talking about? In the same way that Balaam's donkey could see the angel and Balaam couldn't, changing our DNA could change the world that we think we live in. In the next chapter, we will fully explore how a spiritual veil in our perceptions could be opened or closed. Here is an example that happened in one of the trials by AstraZeneca.

"They've Killed God; I Can't Feel God Anymore— My Soul Is Dead" After the Vaccine

- https://beforeitsnews.com/prophecy/2020/09/theyve-killed-god-i-cant-feel-god-anymore-my-soul-is-dead-after-the-vaccine-urgent-read-2514214.html?fbclid=IwAR3nVNZGeCXg1_SjmswXoc9UqWzQwA9HUyuYjntaGf7b4Un4RZ4JKYQQebg

Not only can our spiritual eyes be opened or closed, but splicing reptilian or wolf DNA into a human being would allow a super soldier to be able to kill more easily and with less remorse. Opening up our DNA for anyone to tamper with becomes the Pandora's box that should not be opened. Consequently, genetic manipulation is a crime against humanity, and it is now happening around the globe under a banner of fear.

The Great Deception

The problem that I have with many in the field of Bible prophecy is that they are always telling us what is going to happen. I will be the first to tell you that I do not know what is going to happen or even what the MOB will look like when it happens. I believe we must base our speculation on what we see happening (Luke 21). Unfortunately, many times over the past 18 months, I have wondered what planet are these people living on? All I see is business as usual, as we try and stay away from anything political. Unfortunately, none of this is going to convince some people.

I've had friends of mine tell me, "I'm sorry, Kevan, you're never going be able to convince me that the mark of the beast has anything to do with vaccines." But honestly, this only proves my point that vaccines would be the perfect way to get access to our bodies. People aren't looking for it because the narrative is established. They have had many vaccines before, and they didn't turn into green-eyed monsters. In fact, it doesn't even matter that this isn't a vaccine. But Christians are not the only ones to be alarmed at the idea of changing any of our genetic codes, and many doctors have risked everything to blow the trumpet.

The War of the Seeds

Unfortunately, most Christians are not aware of the parts of the Bible that talk about genetic manipulation, but this idea is clearly hinted at in the first prophecy in the Bible, which is Genesis 3:16. This verse talks about a war between two offspring or seeds, which is why I call it the "War of the Seeds." God says to Adam, Eve, and Satan, "I will put enmity (make enemies, open hostility, war) between you and the woman, and between your seed (offspring) and her Seed; He shall [fatally] bruise your head, and you shall [only] bruise His heel" (AMP).

The seed that fatally wounds Satan is prophetic of the coming of the Messiah, who is the "seed or offspring" of a woman, which was fulfilled through the virgin birth. Still, people do not look at this verse as God telling us Satan's strategy in this war. Satan was going to have offspring in order to defeat God's children. If we understand the envy that Satan has against God, then it is easy to understand why he wants to emulate everything God does, which includes having children. But honestly, Satan needs a lot of help because he also seems to be hopelessly outnumbered (Revelations 12:4).

This passage certainly does define our reality as a battle for the souls of humanity, but does someone giving their soul to Satan completely fulfill this passage? I don't believe that it does. This passage says that Satan's greatest plan is to have offspring that will help him wage this war against God's children. The problem is, where are Satan's literal seed or offspring? An even more fundamental question is how could Satan have literal children, and how could he make the necessary genetic changes to make his dreams come true?

Days of Noah

Fortunately, we don't have to look very long for Satan's offspring because Genesis 6 stands out as the strangest story in the Bible. While even this passage doesn't fully explain how Satan can have seed or offspring, the Nephilim are the only real candidates because they are the only thing different that show up after the six days of creation. Now I am not here to tell us that I know whether disobedient angels can have sex with women and produce offspring, but I am not sure that is absolutely what the text says. More importantly, if I can take a swab of anyone's DNA and have a baby with them, then why are we limiting Satan technologically?

What I get from the passage is quite simple. Human women were taken by fallen angels. These "Sons of God" did not marry these women, and there certainly was no wedding. They did not seem to keep them for very long either. When the women came back, they were pregnant. Later, they gave birth to children that were different in every way. The powers of these Nephilim were the thing of legends. In fact, most all cultures share the stories of how the gods fathered human hybrids. But the obvious implication most of us have missed is that to be that different, Nephilim must have had different DNA. What could have changed their DNA?

Whatever these fallen angels did to produce new offspring, the Bible says that God punished them for it by putting them in an underground prison to be held for judgment (2 Peter 2:4 and Jude 1:6). While the Nephilim were very different, they could still breed with humans, which means they were hybrids. Essentially, if they were left unchecked, these genetic aberrations would have contaminated God's entire creation. God's imagers would have been destroyed because our DNA determines how we look and so much more.

Considering that the Messiah was to come from the "seed of the woman," this was an act of war by anyone's standards. Consequently, God had to intervene to keep the Messianic line uncorrupted. Can you imagine Jesus with gills? Incidentally, genetic integrity is why Noah was chosen because he was "perfect in his generations" (Genesis 6:9). Another hint to the problem is made when God said He destroyed the world with a flood because all flesh had become corrupt (Genesis 6:12). Taking this literally means that their DNA also became corrupt.

Still, if the Nephilim were Satan's offspring, were they at war with humans? The Bible teaches that they were. While the flood took care of most of the Nephilim, somehow, they returned. But that was not to last. They were to be killed everywhere they were found (Deuteronomy 2:10-11, 2:21, and 3:11). These specific passages have become notorious with critics of the Bible because they have allowed them to say that God of the Bible could not possibly be a God of love to do such things.

But if we understand that God said this would happen, then all of this starts to make sense. Understanding that different seeds produce different offspring is an important theme from the very beginnings of our faith. Only in modern times have we been able to understand the genetic implications of these passages. The fact that the Nephilim were better than humans in many ways is a strong indicator of who their father was. After all, it was Satan that first told us he could turn us into gods. This first temptation of the Bible is still the most powerful one today. However, with modern technology, it may not be an empty promise. Transhumanism could turn us all into super-soldiers. The problem is they don't sound that super to me.

The DNA Wars

Why is all of this important? Jesus specifically tells us that just before He returns, it would be just like the days of Noah (DON) (Matthew 24:37). No matter what really happened in Genesis 6, the Nephilim narrative becomes the distinguishing feature of the DON. Can it then be a coincidence that in modern terms, genetic manipulation in the form of transhumanism is once again producing a new offspring with different DNA? Their mistake the first time was to make these hybrids too different. They are not likely to make the same mistake this time, which means they might look just like us.

Keep in mind, this is an age-old war, and God had to intervene the last time, which is why He will again. But this time, He is coming back in person. Consequently, one of the obvious signs that we are in the end times would be the rise of genetic manipulation. Combine the DON with the "super sign," which is that Israel has taken its place in the world, and it is not hard to see why we could be getting close to the return of Jesus (Zechariah 12:3). So what we have to piece together is that the MOB is likely to have a clear connection to the genetic implications of Genesis 3:16 and Genesis 6.

Fortunately, there is yet another passage that helps us tie these concepts together, and it also maintains there will be two kinds of people in the last days. I am talking about the "Divided Kingdom" found in Daniel 2. Recall we are talking about the image with the head of gold followed by silver, bronze, iron, and then the final kingdom. This final kingdom was unique because it was a "divided kingdom" with two distinct kinds of people. Partly iron and partly clay, in that "they mingled themselves with the seed of men, and the two would not mix" (Daniel 2:43).

Who are "they?" One would have to say that the best candidates would have to be the same beings that mingled our genetic material the last time—the disobedient angels who were punished for what they did in the DON. Again, hybrid people with mingled seed certainly make us think of the Nephilim. Indeed, the DON was also characterized by two kinds of people with two different kinds of seed. Just like the last time, the two will not get along. This inherent racism is why it may be prophetic that the National Institutes of Health granted $773,000 to Case Law School to help determine "ethically acceptable rules" for how to integrate human hybrids into our society. In doing so, they recognize that a new level of racism will emerge like never before.

- https://www.christianpost.com/news/listening-to-the-transhumanists.html

Of course, the biggest complaint against some of the narratives involving the Nephilim is the lack of physical evidence. This is where I believe there is a provable cover-up. Some of this cover-up is detailed in the movie, *A Race of Giants*. The movie is told far from a religious point of view. Nonetheless, the movie documents that in America alone, there have been over 1,500 newspaper accounts that have referenced 3,781 skeletons of a race of blond-haired giants (7-12 feet tall).

Recently, LA Marzulli has documented many of the elongated skulls from Peru and shown that they have different DNA. Additionally, their cranial capacity is also approximately 40%

larger, and they have none of the normal cranial sutures of a human skull. (See the Watcher Series: Expert Analysis: DNA results) Still, many of us might be asking ourselves why is changing our genetic codes such a big problem?

The Kinsman Redeemer

For it is not possible that the blood of bulls and goats should take away sins (Hebrews 10:4).

Animals cannot redeem humans. As we have previously said, it was the humanness of Jesus that allowed Him to redeem us. Essentially, Jesus is our kinsman. Jesus would be the first one redeemed to heaven, which is a higher reality of love, holiness, and joy unspeakable. Even though that higher reality has been watching over us and cheering for us, there was no way that we could have ever redeemed ourselves. Even though heaven is a place of love, it cannot compromise itself and allow evil to enter back in (Revelation 21:27). Indeed, no man was good enough until Jesus.

Jesus's disciples called him "good" (Mark 10:18). Because Jesus was God, He was able to be the unblemished Lamb and take away the sins of the whole world. Even more glorious, Jesus now sits on the throne of heaven. What people forget (and what Dr. Michael Heiser points out) is that there is a government in heaven that includes divine courts and counsels. The point is that the death, burial, and resurrection of Jesus destroyed the legal obstacles preventing the reinstatement of our birthright as children of God.

If we were to argue the rights of a father to his son here on earth, most likely the court would order a DNA test. If the father has no common alleles, then that father would have no paternal rights. This is because in our way of thinking, the father is also partly the creator of the child, but only if part of the father's codes are also in his child. Now, I am not trying to say that our DNA saves us, but it is part of who we are and why we look like our Father and bear His image.

On the other hand, we are not just spiritual beings. Even though we are born again of the spirit, our bodies are saved as well. Indeed, all saints who have gone on before us are waiting expectantly for the day when they get their bodies back (Romans 8:23). The mistake is to think of our bodies as only a box we live in as if they don't have anything to do with who we are. The reason the saints groaned is that without their bodies, they were incomplete. Our bodies are part of our identity, and they give us a way to connect and express ourselves in the physical world. Essentially, our bodies are part of our triune nature.

God Wrote Our DNA

If the word of God is sharper than any sword, then what is it about God's words that makes them so powerful? There are many possible answers, but the one I am looking for is that words relay information. If they come from God, they communicate correct information or truth. As we know from scripture, it is the truth that sets us free from the lies of Satan. More importantly, the right words or truth are more powerful at creating a right relationship with God than any other commodity.

Here is the parallel. Just like words, DNA is an information system. But unlike words, DNA also has the ability to change the physical reality of the user. This is why God has specifically commanded that we not mix species (Leviticus 19:198). If we change DNA in any species, then we are changing what God created, which means we are playing God. We are also changing the image from something that God had previously called "good" into something less good. Clearly, we are not capable of making something better than God.

When I think about changing anything God did or said, I like to remember that if God said something different, all of reality would change. God never changes because if He did, He would be less holy, righteous, and loving. This is also why changing any part of what God created is wrong in general. However, when it is directed at changing our DNA, I believe it is blasphemy. After all, this is how God feels when we change the words of the Bible (Revelation 22:18-19).

If God wrote our DNA, then our DNA is relaying correct information. However, if we change our DNA, we are changing the truth of God's creation into a lie. We are choosing to change our very identity at a fundamental level. If we change our DNA, then whose children would we be? If Satan has been planning on having more children since Genesis 3, how far do you think he has gotten since then? More importantly, how far can we go and still be human or still related to Adam or Jesus? Only the courts of heaven could ever know, and I don't intend on finding out.

Blaspheming the Temple of the Holy Spirit

While it is common for Christians to teach that our bodies are "the temple of the Holy Spirit," it is not common for them to realize that every measurement of that temple is determined by the information found in our DNA. Historically, changing the dimensions or any part of the temple would all be considered blasphemy. Now consider that the other unforgivable sin is blaspheming the Holy Spirit, which is denying the ultimate truth that "Jesus is Lord."

> *He who believes in Him is not condemned; but he who does not believe is condemned already, because he has not believed in the name of the only begotten Son of God* (John 3:17-18 NKJV).

> *And all that dwell upon the earth shall worship him, whose names are not written in the book of life of the Lamb slain from the foundation of the world* (Revelation 13:8 NKJV; also see 2 Thessalonians 2:9-12).

Here we see a connection between the people who worship the

beast and their rejection of the Lamb of God. This rejection is a deal-breaker for all of heaven. After all, three simple words, "Jesus is Lord," are the most important and utterly undeniable facts of the universe. However, this information is still something that only the Holy Spirit can reveal to us. If we deny the truth of Jesus, it is difficult to understand how someone can be saved because they have repeatedly blasphemed the witness of the Holy Spirit. Keep in mind just how important the Holy Spirit is in our lives because Jesus said that it was better for Him to leave so that the Holy Spirit could come and live inside of us.

If the Holy Spirit cannot come inside us, then we have blasphemed His temple. On the other hand, through the power of the Holy Spirit, we can walk and talk with God every day in the garden of our hearts. However, no matter how much God loves us, not following His instructions or correct information is what caused Adam and Eve to sin in the first place. The same is also true for Cain. Not following the instructions for the measurements of the temple of the Holy Spirit could cause God to refuse to inhabit it. Changing or destroying God's temple is dangerous because God promises to destroy anyone who dares to do that.

> *Do you not know that you are God's temple and that God's Spirit dwells in you? If anyone destroys God's temple, God will destroy him. For God's temple is holy, and you are that temple* (1 Corinthians 3:16-17 NKJV)

Verses like this have made me ask myself some tough questions. How is it possible to change my DNA and not destroy God's temple? If God refused to inhabit a temple that was not what He instructed or designed, then why wouldn't this also apply to our bodies? Can a Holy God inhabit an unholy temple constructed in direct disobedience? Can a holy God inhabit the unholy seed or offspring of Satan who is created in Satan's image? Did the death of Jesus redeem the seed of Satan? Remember, God hates sin, lies, and hate. So, how could God love or inhabit a being created based on lies, sin, and hate?

These kinds of questions have caused me to believe that all of the unforgivable sins are connected. I believe the MOB is also blaspheming the Holy Spirit because it defiles or destroys the temple of the Holy Spirit, which is our body. This mark appears to make the person uninhabitable. Vice versa, Satan also wants to make a person that he or his demons can inhabit. Remember, Satan's demons appear to be all disembodied spirits, which means they are looking for a body to inhabit so they can express themselves in the world.

This is why we cannot worship God and Satan. There is a choice that has to be made, and that is why people must choose either God or the MOB. What seems logical to me is that if someone changed their DNA enough, then they could have defiled the temple of God. They have destroyed their own body and corrupted the image that they were made in. They also permanently become seed or offspring of the one who offered them this change. Furthermore, it would be difficult to imagine how the Holy Spirit could inhabit the children of Satan.

It may also be important to remember that the promise of transhumanism is to remake mankind into a new image. But God doesn't want us in any other image. God wants us to allow him to restore our image but not change it. Now consider the Covid cause is forcing us to take something that has never been proposed in modern history—the idea of overwriting our mRNA so that we no longer follow some of God's instructions. Who in their right mind would want to do that, but it is happening. Unfortunately, both political parties in America are pushing it as the solution to the problem. The only difference is that some of them are saying it should be mandatory.

Enter the Alien Agenda

As if I haven't pushed the envelope enough, I am still going further because there is an obvious connection. Few are willing to talk about it, but I will point out how this phenomenon is manifesting some of the exact same narratives of this book. Why aren't we talking about aliens? After all, more Americans now believe in aliens more than God. (See below.) That statistic alone should be a strong indicator as to how the Antichrist might best present himself to the world as its true savior. So, how can we not talk about that? After all, the things we don't talk about are the things that would enable the world to hear another side of the story.

• https://entertainment.ie/trending/statistics-show-that-more-people-believe-in-ghosts-and-aliens-than-god-342325/

Not only is the TV show *Ancient Aliens* popular, but much of it can also be easily debunked. (See below.) However, even some basic investigation on the alien hypothesis can yield some startling intersections with biblical themes. For instance, there is a movie on Amazon Prime called, *Extraordinary: The Seeding*. Not only does this movie have multiple accounts of women being abducted by aliens and coming back pregnant, but the name of it, "The Seeding," is the same word the Bible used to describe what Satan will one day have.

• https://youtu.be/j9w-i5oZqaQ

Later, many of these same women are abducted again before giving birth, and this time the baby is taken. However, some of these women are re-abducted and even meet their children. Okay, so what does this sound like? This scenario is almost the same one talked about in Genesis 6. The difference seems to be that they have learned a few things since then. Meaning, they don't let the baby be born because that might make world news.

Whether we believe in alien abduction or not, they have several connection points with some of the supernatural things found in the Bible. One example is when angels helped Peter escape prison. Just as Peter's cuffs fell off, people could pass through other solid objects. Like Peter's guards, sometimes people are paralyzed and can't move. The shocking thing is that the people in the UFO community teach that once an abduction starts, it cannot be stopped. But this isn't true.

A man by the name of Joe Jordan, a MUFON certified investigator, has documented hundreds of cases where the name of Jesus stopped aliens' abductions in their tracks. Now, what does that sound like? It sounds like we should be teaching that from every pulpit in the country. Through this discovery, Joe not only became a Christian, but he now helps people see the connection between the alien agenda and demons. He also sees a connection with Satan's desire to have offspring.

- https://youtu.be/NuMajWp_EzA &
  https://www.youtube.com/watch?v=BOC7K3L86TM

But Joe Jordan is not the only one. Dr. David Jacobs is the author of *UFO Controversy in America, Secret Life: Firsthand Accounts of UFO Abductions, and The Threat*. Dr. Jacobs has been studying alien abductions for longer than probably anyone (30+ years). In an interview, Dr. Jacobs was asked what alien abductions have in common. He said it was their "obsession with genetic material." When asked what he made of that, he replied, they have their "own breeding program." Now, what does that sound like?

The only thing that stops these entities is the name of Jesus, and they are obsessed with genetic material because they probably have a breeding program. Could this be why the world is going so crazy so fast? We always talk about our spiritual warfare with spiritual powers and principalities, but could there be a literal seed of Satan already among us? Could this same seed be a way for disembodied demons to manifest themselves into our world and take up the age-old "War of the Seeds?" Again, I cannot say whether this is all true, but I can say that the alien phenomenon clearly has intersections with biblical narratives.

The last thing I will mention about the alien agenda is something that Pastor Billy Crone has brought out in some of his studies on aliens. Billy is a Baptist minister, but previously he was part of the New Age movement. Consequently, he is familiar with remote viewing, astral projection, and out-of-body experiences. But one of my favorite of Pastor Billy's sermons was about how aliens act like demons. Billy even goes on to reveal that many of the New Age authors are channeling their messages from spirits who identify themselves as aliens.

This is important for us to consider. Once the Abyss is opened, the spirits who have been in prison need to have a strategy about how to present themselves to the world. I think it is safe to say that an alien race would be the most logical choice. Now that would certainly be quite the deception, especially when more people now believe in aliens than God.

What God Has, Satan Wants

Just as God desires to have children, Satan also wants to do the same, but he needs them for a far more sinister purpose—to wage war against the children of God. Satan himself was a child of God, and that is why he wants to recruit as many as he can against God. But I also believe that Satan also desires to be a father to children that take after him. The sad reality is that technology is already available for Satan to start that process. If people can channel books, then why can't they write DNA?

This can make the "war of the seeds," and the "days of Noah" happen all over again. Breakthroughs like CRISPR allow people to write new strands of DNA and splice their way towards a new race of beings. Indeed, this current mRNA jab marks the beginning of genetic experimentation on the masses. But it could be much worse than that. Unfortunately, the worldwide cause has blinded us with fear. Yet, none of this deception would be possible if we had not failed to see and know Bible prophecy and the genetic narratives of the Bible.

The Politically Correct Church

When we see Jesus face to face, we will look like Him and be like Him (1 John 3:2). How would that meeting go if we didn't look like Him? If DNA determines how we look, then how can anyone claim that overwriting (what God wrote) our natural RNA or DNA is somehow godly? This vaccine, by all appearances, is the start of changing what God wrote when He made us.

Consequently, we have no idea what kinds of doors we are opening up. There is little room to debate that we are not officially messing with the code of life and playing God in the process. Unfortunately, churches see this subject as a medical or political issue, so they steer clear of it as if it will go away. But not all churches are being silent. Some are speaking the truth, which is that our Bibles are happening.

Already, people have to face a difficult decision that challenges their faith and their rights to their own body. They feel trapped and alone. How can we not help them? After all, love cannot sit and do nothing while our choices are being taken away. Unfortunately, we are already at a point where we must peacefully defy our government and its mandates. Remember, Jesus was killed for political reasons and because He refused to comply. How can we expect anything different in the end times?

Our society has broken with its Christian heritage. Consequently, a day is coming very soon when people will no longer be able to believe what they see on TV or hear in the media and still be Christian. The false Covid narrative has already emptied our churches, and the next great cause will be even worse. We who are mature in the Lord must begin to prepare those we can for this break with our society. We are now only a small sub-culture or counter-culture.

While we can still strive for peace, a war is coming, and we cannot shrink back because we are carrying the truth down to our DNA. We must continue to stand up for the Great Commission of our Lord. Just with one small change. Beware of the mark of the beast! Do not give up access to your body lightly. If we heed His commands, we have a promise from the Lord. He will be with us "always, even unto the end of the age" (Matthew 28:20).

6

The Coming War of Spirits

The Opening of the Abyss

Then the fifth angel sounded: And I saw a star fallen from heaven to the earth. To him was given the key to the bottomless pit. And he opened the bottomless pit, and smoke arose out of the pit like the smoke of a great furnace. So, the sun and the air were darkened because of the smoke of the pit. Then out of the smoke locusts came upon the earth. And to them was given power, as the scorpions of the earth have power. They were commanded not to harm the grass of the earth, or any green thing, or any tree, but only those men who do not have the seal of God on their foreheads (Revelation 9:1-4 NKJV).

While I have stated that I believe the MOB is Satan's master plan, I have often wondered why he didn't do it sooner. Certainly, technology could have something to do with it, but there is also a key that God must give back for all of this to happen. Vice versa, there is also a key that we must not give back, which is the key to our bodies. The reason is that something mysterious is coming—an opening of sorts. An underground prison full of disobedient spirits will be released on humanity for the second time. Of course, some of the mystery is furthered because these spirits were punished for what they did in the days of Noah.

But for the Abyss to open, the restrainer has to be taken out of the way. What do you think these spirits are going to do when they are released? Probably the same thing they did the last time. We just don't know exactly what. But the good news is that they do not have free reign. God's seal is going to be applied to the foreheads of many people, and they cannot tamper with them. We have to keep in mind that Satan has most likely marked the foreheads of his followers. The people who have taken the MOB have a stamp, a brand, or a unique identifier that targets them for demonic oppression or possession.

The idea of something marking our foreheads is not that foreign in the Bible. For example, in Revelation 17, there is a woman who has something written on her forehead: "Babylon the Great, the Mother of Harlots and of the Abominations of the Earth." Later, in Revelation 13:6, the deceived children of this same harlot also receive a mark on their foreheads (Revelation 14:9). One would have to think this is also the MOB.

Things being written on our foreheads could also be referring to the idea that our minds are an open book in heaven, and they can be read just like we read a book. After all, nothing can be hidden in the spiritual realm (Mark 4:22). Consequently, these marks on our forehead may be a sign of what is inside of our minds and our hearts. Having Satan in complete control of our minds and our hands could also easily correlate with the idea of a seared conscience (1 Timothy 4:2).

Marks and Seals on Our Foreheads

As we have said, these marks are not necessarily literal or visible in the physical realm, but they are giant flashing billboards in the spiritual world, and they cannot be missed. For example, God's children also have something written on their foreheads. Think of Revelation 14:1 and how it speaks of the 144,000 who have both the name of the Lamb and the Father written on their foreheads.

These kinds of passages let us know that when we are talking about a mark on our foreheads, we could be talking about symbolism, imagery, or just a physical description of spiritual things. Another reason Revelation 9 is important is because the opening of the Abyss represents the moment when the spirit of the Antichrist is released upon the world for the second time. This spirit is already the king over all the other spirits in the Abyss. He is called a (fallen) angel of the bottomless pit; in the "Hebrew tongue (it) is *Abaddon* but in the Greek tongue his name *Apollyon*" (Revelation 9:11).

What is also important is that "(Jesus) went and preached to the spirits in prison, who disobeyed long ago when God waited patiently in the days of Noah while the ark was being built" (1 Peter 3:19-20). I believe Jesus witnessed to them that He now holds all power in heaven, on earth, and of the underworld. Since then, Jesus has been holding the key to the Abyss and restraining the satanic hosts. What might be shocking for most of us is that Jesus is going to give it back to Satan one last time. Then and only then can Satan open up the Abyss and regain his captured troops.

But of all the spirits Satan hopes to retain, the spirit of the Antichrist is the most important. The fact that this spirit comes out of the Abyss means that he has been here before and was punished for what he did then. This is also true of all the other spirits coming out of the Abyss. This time they will have 1000s of years of pent-up rage to unleash upon the world. Reading all of Revelations 9 reveals that the beings coming out of the Abyss are also human-beast hybrids, which gives us insight into the genetic aspirations of Satan.

Unfortunately, they are given great power, but they do not have free reign over the earth. These weird creatures cannot hurt the grass and the trees. They also cannot kill, but they can torment. Most importantly, before these spirits are released, an angel puts a seal on the forehead of all God's children to stop the evil spirits from tormenting them. From my perspective, it cannot be a coincidence that in the end times both Satan and God seal all of their children with a mark or seal on their foreheads. But it is the description of the opening of the Abyss that helps us understand how each mark or seal works.

Disembodied Spirits

All of this imagery is important for us to see that evil spirits or demons are the ones coming out of the Abyss. They may not have bodies, so they will be looking for a body to take over, inhabit, or possess. Again, if the main goal of God is to inhabit us with His Holy Spirit, then wouldn't the main goal of Satan be to possess our bodies with his demons? This is what demonic possession is all about.

We also have to remember that being disembodied may not be very comfortable or satisfying. After all, spirits have limited ways of interacting with the physical world. Disembodied spirits, ghosts, and demons are real, but not having a body inhibits them (Luke 24:37).

The opening of the Abyss represents the exact point that the spirit who is the Antichrist actually takes possession of his host. Therefore, it is likely that the MOB must be fully in play by this point so that these other unholy spirits can possess their targets as well.

This return of an ancient spirit makes sense because the Antichrist is described as one of seven kings who would also be an eighth king (Revelation 17:6-12). Remember, the Antichrist is someone "who was, and is not, and who will be." It says it three times because it is that important and hard to believe because we are talking about a cycle of repeated possession. The question is, does this idea of bodies being separated from spirits hold up? The Bible specifically says that if we are absent from the body, we are present with the Lord. (2 Corinthians 5:8)

Additionally, the Greek word (*Oiketerion*) for the new body we get when we are resurrected (2 Corinthians 5:3) happens to be the same word for what the fallen angels lost in the heavenly war (Jude

1:6). Essentially our body or house is the dwelling place for our spirit, and a seal on our forehead represents a barrier to demons entering. This idea explains why these disobedient spirits can only torment those without Godly seals in their foreheads. But the question then becomes, if one seal keeps one spirit in and keeps the other out, then why isn't this true of MOB? After all, Satan's seal is also on the forehead. This would certainly explain why we cannot be saved once we have taken the MOB.

All of this imagery allows us to see how our foreheads could be considered a gateway or door whereby spirits can enter our body. Indeed, it is the mark or seal on the door that determines who can enter. Most importantly, it is the Holy Spirit that writes the name of God Himself in our foreheads. In this sense, the Holy Spirit is also the restrainer. When we become inhabited by the Holy Spirit, we become temples of the living God. Henceforth, we are sealed or pledged until the day of redemption (2 Corinthians 1:21; Revelation 7:3; Ephesians 1:13; and Ephesians 4:30). This same seal will take the saints through the tribulation, even though many of them will be lost (Revelations 6:10 and 20:4).

Ancient Aliens?

Sorry, but I have to go there one more time. The idea that spirits or ancient entities will be released has always caused me to ask an intriguing question: How will they represent themselves to the world upon their return? Honestly, there aren't that many options. They can't say they are demons just fresh out of an underground prison. That's when it hit me. The most logical way to reveal themselves, based upon most people's worldview, would be as aliens.

Think about the show *Ancient Aliens*. In the introduction, they ask, "Who were they? Where did go? When will they return?" Here is the answer to all three questions. They are demons or fallen angels. They left because God put them in prison for what they did in the days of Noah. In the last days, they will return when the key to the Abyss is given back to Satan. When I think about the Abyss, I tend to think of it as another dimension. Consequently, I find it very interesting that the stated purpose of the large Hadron Collider or CERN is to "open a doorway to another dimension." Through this open door, something might come through, or we might send something through.

Could modern technology also be part of how this doorway to the underworld is opened? Finally, we also need to realize that the last time a portal to another dimension was going to be opened, God intervened, and that was at the Tower of Babel. Could CERN be how the Abyss is opened and does this hidden agenda to release Satan's troops go all the way back to the Tower of Babel, the birthplace of Babylon? Could all of these events be part of the hidden agenda of Mystery Babylon described in Revelation 18?

- https://www.christianevidence.net/2019/05/cern-and-bible-prophecy.html

Connecting the Dots

So, let's summarize what we have learned so far. Essentially, all of our Bible passages have broken things down into two distinct categories. The question is: are they all related?

PROPHETIC PASSAGES	SAVED/WORSHIP GOD	UNSAVED/WORSHIP SATAN
War of the Seed (Gen. 3)	God's Seed or Offspring	Satan's Seed or Offspring
Days of Noah (Gen. 6)	Noah was perfect in his generations and was saved	Nephilim/hybrid humans had corrupt flesh and were destroyed
Divided Kingdom or Last Kingdom of Daniel 2	Un-mingled Seed	Mingled Seed
Mark of the Beast (Rev. 13)	Unmarked Foreheads	Marked Foreheads
Opening of Abyss (Rev. 9)	Foreheads Sealed for the Holy Spirit	Foreheads Sealed for Satan

The first three prophetic passages leave us with the distinct impression that genetic material is being changed unless you are prepared to spiritualize the entire narrative. But spiritualization doesn't explain two different kinds of people or offspring. Also, how could they be so different if they didn't have different DNA? Remember, Goliath's brothers had six fingers and six toes. So, the next question becomes, Is it possible that there is also a genetic connection to the MOB and the sealing or unsealing of our foreheads? I believe it is.

We are specifically told the last days will be like the DON, which means the DON and the MOB are manifesting simultaneously. After all, the idea of a genetic marker (with its spiritual implications) could fulfill the general parameters of the MOB, especially if those genetic changes crossed the blood-brain barrier of our mind. Indeed, the redemption of humanity through Jesus Christ is species specific. If we became another fallen species, we could not be saved (Hebrews 10:4).

What we want to explore now is the idea that all of these things are connected. For example, it would also make sense that upon the release of the demons of the Abyss that they could more easily possess the seed of Satan. While genetic changes could change who we are related to, they could also change how our mind works or how our spirit is sealed within our body. They could also explain why a satanically marked forehead cannot then be sealed by God.

We have already detailed how altering our DNA might also alter how we act, how our minds work, and our very nature. Consequently, it is not that far-fetched to think that changing us genetically could change our perception of reality. We may perceive things differently. We might also see and experience things that we never have before.

Remember, Balaam's donkey could see the angel, but Balaam could not. These genetic differences between Balaam and his donkey could certainly be described as sealed or unsealed concerning what they each perceive in the spiritual realm. In essence, we have the power to ignore angels, but the donkey did not. This is all the more reason why a godly seal or signet is needed to prevent demonic possession after the opening of the Abyss.

In contrast, the MOB represents being open to Satan and being closed to God. This is the point at which humanity will be sorted and marked as either a sheep or a goat by their respective fathers. A satanic seal on our foreheads is exactly what the mark of the beast appears to be. This opening to demonic forces would also explain why the people who worship the beast are the ones who take his mark. Indeed, the demons in the Abyss have already been worshiping this same king for millennia.

Their minds have been changed to see Satan as their god. In doing so, their conscience has been seared, and they have made their final choice. Hence, the Holy Spirit can no longer reach them or inhabit them. Just as we are purchased with a price, their souls are also claimed by Satan's rights as their father and creator.

Opening or Closing the Veil

The idea of a seal could also work like a veil to our mind that can be opened or closed. Think of the Holiest of Holies in the temple of Jerusalem. When the veil was rent from top to bottom, it symbolized that God's dwelling place was once again in our hearts, and we no longer needed an intercessor between God and man. The barrier was destroyed, and once again, God could dwell inside of our body.

This same opening to the Holy Spirit also came with a closed veil or seal with regard to certain amounts of demonic influence and tampering. For the most part, God's seal or veil presides over the lives of a Christian all the way to salvation, thus preventing complete demonic possession along the way. This does not mean that Christians will never need some deliverance from spiritual oppression, as many of us can attest. But the difference is we have been sealed by the Holy Spirit for redemption. While salvation is a done deal, this same seal by the Holy Spirit also helps us recognize the MOB and strengthens us so that we don't take it.

And do not grieve the Holy Spirit of God, with whom you were sealed for the day of redemption (Ephesians 4:30 NIV).

The Mystery of the MOB

Now reverse this principle. Is there a seal of Satan that can prevent someone from changing their mind about Jesus and repenting? The Bible says that there is, and it is called the MOB. This mark seals the forehead of someone to the domain of Satan and prevents God from being able to save them. Thinking about the imagery of the Abyss, God's seal in the forehead does the same thing because Satan has no power over them. In this way, the MOB and the sealing or unsealing of the forehead are two parts of the same puzzle.

An open, unsealed, or unstable mind is why the people who take the MOB are the same people who worship all that is beastly. Consequently, a seal in the forehead, one way or another, represents two distinct features of the end times, and they appear to be intricately related. Knowing that this sealing of the foreheads occurs during a repeat of the days of Noah (Genesis 3 and 6), we have a big hint that the MOB and the unsealed mind may have something to do with genetic manipulation.

The divided Kingdom of Daniel 2 also gives testimony about how the last kingdom on earth would have two kinds of people—mingled seed people and unmingled seed people. These genetic markers could explain why someone who chooses to take this mark could not be saved. While all of us have the potential to become God's children, it is our choice whether to follow Jesus that determines our fate. Somehow, choosing to take the MOB is doing the same thing, which is why God has warned us about it 2000 years in advance. What cannot be missed is that humanity has never had the choice to change our DNA before.

Furthermore, if our genetic information becomes blasphemy, why wouldn't our minds, our temples, and our words also become blasphemy? Essentially, changing our genetics could change who we are to the point that we are no longer what God created, which is why our genetic material is sacred. I realize this is complicated, but I think the Covid conspiracy is worthy of his cunning craftiness (John 8:44). Consequently, now is the time to stand up and reach out to everyone struggling to make a choice.

The Bindi and the Tilak

As we think about what a mark on the forehead could be, it cannot be overlooked that faiths such as Hinduism, Buddhism, and Jainism actually put a dot on their forehead. Respectively, the Bindi is for married women, and the Tilak is usually for men. Both of these marks represent the opening of the "third eye," which represents their spiritual eyes, or we could call them "donkey eyes." Not only does this new sight allow them to see into the spiritual world, but it also allows them to interact with the spirits who are there. In some cases, it is this interaction that can also lead to demonic possession.

Historically, these marks represent the point at which creation begins, and everything is united, which is the fusion of our individuality with the universal consciousness. This universalist concept is also symbolized by a mandala. Becoming one with the universe is the specific goal of all meditation, but it is also symbolic of something called a "Kundalini Awakening." In case you were wondering, the "Kundalini" is a coiled serpent. The serpent coils itself around the spine until it bites down on something on our foreheads.

Traditionally, this is thought to be the pineal gland. This is not a lot to go on, but a fringe experiment used magnets placed on the forehead to stimulate the pineal gland. This was done by Dr. Walter Rawls, and it produced some ghostly visions and interactions. Either way, there are things available, such as mind-altering drugs and radio frequencies, that can open us up to some very bad trips, and some very ugly demonic forces. There are also reports of how modern technology can interfere with how the brain works, including our memories and even our relationship with God.

- https://arizonaparanormalresearch.com/2017/11/06/the-pineal-gland-magnet-experiment/

- https://shepherdsheart.life/blogs/news/hydrogel-quantum-dot-can-erase-your-memory-of-god-and-his-creation

- https://mypatriotsnetwork.com/patriot/hydrogel-darpa-vaccines-oh-my/

The Most Famous Third Eye

Of course, the most famous "third eye" on the planet is on our one-dollar bill. Knowing that bill is a masonic trestle board (a visual business plan) allows us to see that there are a group of people who have been here since the founding of our country that are behind this conspiracy. What you see on your one-dollar bill is their intention for America, but God still has His purposes for us that cannot be thwarted.

If we still think there is nothing spiritual about our foreheads, then why do we anoint people on their foreheads when we pray for them? Symbolically, the oil represents the Holy Spirit. This tradition sheds light on the idea that our enemy might have an agenda hidden on our foreheads.

As we have previously said, the MOB may represent a metamorphosis of our minds. Could this be the reason why Goliath defied the armies of Israel? Could this also be the reason that the minds of those in the days of Noah were "evil continually?" We have mentioned how these mRNA codes could be marking our brains because they are crossing the blood-brain barrier.

Not only do these supposed vaccines not do what all vaccines do, they do something no other vaccine has ever done—they widely distribute themselves throughout the body within hours. This is huge because normally, vaccines remain close to the vaccination site. The question then becomes, what effect do these spike pathogens have on the rest of our bodies?

- https://rightsfreedoms.wordpress.com/2021/06/16/researcher-we-made-a-big-mistake-on-covid-19-vaccine/

Opening the Third Eye

I have thought about the implications of being sealed or unsealed against demonic influence and possession for quite some time. I have also thought about how all of these ideas seem to be connected. But what I want to expound upon is the idea that the occultic world has been working towards these goals since day one. Essentially, demonic possession and influence are the goals of all false religions. What cannot be denied is that spirits do not usually have access to us, so something has to be changed for that to happen.

If the seal of God on our foreheads will protect our minds from the hosts of Satan when they are released, then what do you think the MOB does? (Revelation 7:3). Knowing that the root word used for forehead indicates that a metamorphosis has taken place, all seems to fit. Furthermore, the same word indicates that those who take this mark could be referred to as metahumans. Once again, it leaves us with the idea that we could be talking about human hybrids with superpowers.

After all, the mind, body, spirit connection is the occultic view of who we are. The ultimate identity that the New Age movement promotes comes from this openness and eventual margining with universal consciousness. Hence why the opening of our third eye is the end game of all of Satan's schemes. Most Christians are unaware that the occultic world has been using mind-altering drugs, yoga, and eastern styles of meditation to open our third eye for thousands of years.

Yoga Opens Doors

This story is one of those that is difficult to believe, but I received it firsthand from a patient of mine. He and his entire family are from Italy and mostly Catholic. I can't remember how we got on the topic of demonic possession, but I remember him saying that he never used to believe in that until it happened to his brother. His brother was doing yoga one day, and his instructor walked up to him and touched him on his forehead. This is called a *Shakti Pat*, where one person's energy imparts the opening of someone else's third eye. What happened next was very reminiscent of someone coming unsealed in their forehead.

His brother called him on the way home and told him that it was like he was spiritually raped. Later, he found out that his brother had cried for hours after he got home. After that, life kind of went back to normal for a while, at least until the summer when their whole family took a vacation/pilgrimage back to Italy. Once they got there, his brother started acting strange. Soon, the behavior escalated to the point that the police got involved. Now, most people know that you do not want to go to prison in Italy. Luckily, they were able to negotiate a deal with the police.

That's when this man had to spend three days with his brother in a hotel room, trying to restrain him from doing things he shouldn't. It didn't take long for him to realize his brother wasn't just having a psychotic break, his brother was demonically possessed. There was no way to explain the experience of someone you have known your whole life acting and saying the things that his brother did. But as soon as they got on the plane home, his brother started going back to normal.

Now most of us have come to accept the practice of yoga in our society as harmless enough. But there is a spiritual side to yoga. I always used to recommend staying away from the spiritual part of yoga. This means not participating in any kind of Eastern meditation, chanting, or visualizations. The problem is that even the positions or poses are a form of worship within the Hindu religion because they are creating a submissive posture towards one of the Hindu gods. Not only are these poses constantly being rehearsed by the participant, they represent the symbolic worship of pagan gods.

Portals to Our Minds

Another point to make clear is that while the Bible calls us to meditate on God and His words, this is not what is happening with Eastern meditation. The goal of Eastern meditation is to empty one's self to connect with nature, themselves, and the universal consciousness, whoever that is. Meditation, like drugs, can put us in an altered state where we can be influenced and changed by the forces that we are opening ourselves up to. This is the opposite of our call as Christians to memorize scripture, sing songs, pray, and fill ourselves through our relationship and communion with God.

> *Finally, brothers and sisters, whatever is true, whatever is noble, whatever is right, whatever is pure, whatever is lovely, whatever is admirable—if anything is excellent or praiseworthy—think about such things* (Philippians 4:8 NIV).

Steven Bancarz, who was delivered from the New Age cult, has a great video on YouTube called *Proof Meditation Is Dangerous & Demonic*. In the video, he has many explosive excerpts from a mindfulness yoga master by the name of Leo. Leo has a website called actualized.org, and he has more than a million followers. After watching this video, all I can tell you is that it is the opposite of "thinking about excellent things."

It doesn't even fit the idea of mindfulness. If we experience what Leo says we can experience in meditation, we could be talking about full-on demonic possession. Meditation is also instrumental in out-of-body experiences, astral projection, remote viewing, channeling, and remote writing. Here are some excerpts from mindfulness moments with Leo!

> Expect waves of insanity and madness ... Expect depression and meaninglessness ... Expect Suicidal thoughts ... Doing drugs, alcohol ... Expect nightmares ... Expect weird dreams: where you have sex with your mother, killing people, or butchering your dog ... You may start to behave like an animal and howl at the moon ... You may experience paranormal phenomenon: past lives, seeing the future, out-of-body experiences, see spirits, hear weird voices, see angels and demons standing in front of you ... You may see gods ... giant insects ... Experience: entities, aliens, being abducted or probed ... You may experience a Kundalini awakening ... Feel as if you are losing your mind ... Experience weird energy moving through you ... Like you are being controlled by a puppet master ... Almost like you are being demonically possessed.

• https://www.youtube.com/watch?v=T0Sbs0YOGk8

Altered States

Yoga is not the sin of choice to open our spiritual eyes, but the sins of witchcraft and sorcery are. In the Bible, the Greek word for this kind of sin is called *Pharmakeía*, from which we get our English word "pharmacy." Both Shaman and witch doctors have been using mind-altering drugs for millennia to channel thoughts from the mind of Satan and the hearts of demons to their sages, adepts, and illuminated ones. So could some of the fog that has started to descend upon our world be coming from the same source?

This is what is behind the great push to legalize drugs in our country. It is especially true of marijuana because it is the first drug most people use to achieve this kind of altered state of consciousness. Already, America is in the midst of an opioid epidemic. One in six Americans is taking some kind of psychiatric drug, which are mostly antidepressants. Additionally, 31.9 million Americans are on illicit drugs. So maybe this is why something is happening to the minds of Americans.

- https://www.verywellmind.com/rates-of-illicit-drug-abuse-in-the-us-67027

- https://www.nbcnews.com/health/health-news/one-6-americans-take-antidepressants-other-psychiatric-drugs-n695141

Most people would be shocked to know that drugs and New Age churches go together like peas and carrots. This is why "Legal DMT Churches Are Popping Up Across the United States and Canada."

- https://eraoflight.com/2020/09/29/legal-dmt-churches-are-popping-up-across-the-united-states-and-canada/

DMT (N, N-Dimethyltryptamine) is a recreational psychotropic drug used by various cultures to induce alterations in perception, consciousness, cognition, and behavior. They are having success in getting this drug legal for their use because they can make a case that ayahuasca tea, which contains DMT, has been historically used for spiritual development based on ancient texts. Like other mind-altering drugs, DMT can open a portal to our minds so that we can see or interact with the demonic world.

A Seared Conscience

Why do people watch or record someone who needs help, but

they don't actually help them? Why do people pull out their phones, but they don't roll up their sleeves? I am still dumbfounded by the success of YouTube, Facebook, and taking selfies because people would rather watch than participate. People would rather be seen doing something rather than just savor the moment.

But this is only one of a million downward trends. I am personally frightened at how successful horror movies have become, generating 413 million dollars in 2012. People are spending thousands of dollars and hundreds of hours a year watching people being tortured and mutilated for pleasure. We all know that gore, violence, and sex have taken over the TV and movie industry. Both of them allow us to live in a virtual or voyeuristic reality. People are obsessed with avatars, role-playing games, and video games that enable them to go through the motions of virtually every sin on the planet. The pornography industry is larger than we can imagine, and it primarily works the same way.

The point is that something is happening to the conscience of America. How else can they celebrate being able to kill a baby the day before it's born by lighting up buildings in New York City? We have no conscience, and there is no outrage at sin. In fact, it is righteousness that has become outrageous and even illegal. Saving a child from being killed is still applauded, but stepping between a woman and an abortion clinic get us arrested. The battle for what is in our minds and hearts is being tipped toward the doctrine of demons because of everything we have discussed so far.

Unfortunately, these schemes of the devil are way too controversial to ever make it into our sermons. Not only is the church not ready for any tribulation (because we have taught that as an impossibility), they are also not prepared for an outpouring of unholy spirits upon the world. Yet, the Bible maintains that it is an impossibility for the elect to be deceived. However, the implication is that everyone else would. The good news is that we too are promised an outpouring of the Holy Spirit in the last days to counteract the spirits coming from the Abyss (Acts 2:16-21). But of all the things we are not prepared for, no one has told us to prepare to answer the tough questions coming our way.

The Sorting Room

Therefore, everyone who will confess in Me before men, I also will confess in him before My Father in the heavens. And whoever shall deny Me before men, I also will deny him before My Father in the heavens. Do not think that I came to bring peace to the earth; I came not to bring peace, but a sword. For I came to set at variance "A man against his father, and a daughter against her mother, and a daughter-in-law against her mother-in-law, and the enemies of the man are his own household" (Luke 12:49-53 NKJV).

A day is coming when all of humanity will be sorted, but the important part is that it all happens based upon what we say here on earth. Not only will spirits be coming to test the faith of everyone on the face of the earth, but we will be sifted, and we will be shaken (Haggai 2:7). In fact, almost everything I have covered so far has sorted people into two groups. This is because Jesus is the dividing line of history and of our hearts. Consequently, as we see history coming to a close, we have to know that the sheep would eventually be separated from the goats.

While I believe we still need to be peacemakers, there can be no more mincing of words, for our enemy is now fully formed and on the loose. This is only the first of many great causes to come and sort the world's populations. Yet, the Covid narrative is the greatest sorting event I have ever witnessed. Even our last election was a massive sorting event, and we all got schooled. It has been painful to read the articles of Christians who supported Biden now saying that he has betrayed them. The deceived are starting to repent.

But of all the things we have heard this past year that foretells our future was the proposal by some communists, posing as Democrats, that the only thing that could fix our countries problems were "re-education camps." Of course, any similarity to concentration camps is just strictly coincidental. Yet, these are the kinds of things that only a Communist or Nazi could say, and both America and the media tolerated it. This is the goal of the "New World Order." The reality of the communist takeover of America cannot be denied unless you were to hear the sermons still being preached across our lands.

Then one would think things are going along just fine, but this is all pretending. The problem is that the one-world government that the Bible says is coming is consistent with either communism or a dictatorship. So, whether you agree with me about this being the pre-cursor to the MOB, it is impossible to argue that the Covid narrative is not putting into place all the necessary controls that the "beast" government will one day use to bring about the full version of the MOB.

Already, half of Americans are okay with having a vaccine passport even though that would be the end of freedom, democracy, and our rights to our bodies. The administration of this narrative is also a dividing line between those who believe what is on TV and those who believe in their God and their body. When I think about sorting people, this story told by a master Mason came to mind. When they are sorting people for their different degrees, they call them into a room and ask them some simple questions.

The Ultimate Question

Two people are told to spit on a cross. Depending on their response, the test giver comes up with a way of justifying what they did. "I can see by you spitting on this cross that you recognize that on some level this is just a piece of wood. You can go through door number one." Vice versa, "I can see by you refusing to spit on this

155

cross that you are a man that will not compromise on principle. You can go through door number two."

This is exactly what is happening in America. Are you Republican or Democrat? Are you white or black? Are you for or against abortion? Are you willing to be vaccinated or not? Do you believe in mandates or not? One of my great privileges is to serve is as president of the board for soilminstries.org. "Serving Others in Love" is a pipeline of vision and resources to Honduras, which is the second poorest country in our hemisphere. Just a few weeks ago, we were able to book a doctor for a medical mission trip.

When we were wrapping up some of the details with his office manager, she said, "Oh, one last thing. Everyone who goes with us must be vaccinated." I was shocked. Vaccines that admittedly don't work are now literally being used to divide Christians and keep them from even doing charity together. But if we are Christians, then we cannot be for mandatory vaccinations because they require a person to give up access to their temple.

Not only is their body the temple of the Holy Spirit, but a pandemic perfectly fits the cause talked about in the Bible as to how the MOB will be rolled out upon the world. Consequently, if we are going to call ourselves Christians, then we cannot remain silent about Satan's schemes even if they are political schemes. Yet, the time for sorting is here. Souls will be both won and lost. Soon, there will be no more cultural Christians.

Christians will either live by their Bible, or they will perish believing what is on television. The pretending has to stop. Things are not going back to normal. We can no longer pretend that America is not hostile to both freedom and Christianity. The Democratic party is full of communists. They have fully admitted that they plan to add more democratic states and stack the Supreme Court. They are in complete control to the point of eliminating our Constitution, while they completely disregard the freedoms it says we have.

Consequently, every freedom we have is in jeopardy. Virtually everyone in the media is in on it. There is nowhere for any conservative voices of reason to proclaim the truth to our society regarding the error of our ways. All except for one! The church is still here, but it won't be able to do anything unless we continue to allow the government to close our doors and keep what is happening out of our sermons. The time has come for us to come together and say enough is enough.

We must return to preaching the whole of scripture, and that includes Bible prophecy. It is the book called the Bible that has perpetually been unchanged for 1000s of years. That is our only source of truth in these troubled times. The Bible is what we need to make it through the times that are coming. But even more importantly, we need more of God in our lives and a closer, more intimate connection to Him. After all, God has promised us that He will never leave us or forsake us (Hebrews 13:5-6).

7

Discerning the Spirits

Testing the Spirits

The coming of the lawless one will be accompanied by the working of Satan, with every kind of power, sign, and false wonder (2 Thessalonians 2:9 BSB).

And it shall come to pass in the last days, says God, that I will pour out of My Spirit on all flesh; your sons and your daughters shall prophesy, your young men shall see visions, your old men shall dream dreams. And on My menservants and My maid-servants, I will pour out of My Spirit in those days; and they shall prophesy. I will show wonders in Heaven above and signs in the earth beneath (Acts 2:16-21 KJV).

So many game-changers are coming, and unfortunately, Christians are woefully behind in addressing these issues. The biggest question I have is, when the spirits come out of the Abyss, are we wholly prepared for all of the stories they will tell everyone? The imagery of the "opening of the Abyss" lets us know that the end times will be characterized by an outpouring of spirits. These spirits are going to come with crazy lies and supernatural wonders to back them up. The problem is, how are we going to tell which spirits are which? Of course, we will still need the helper or the Holy Spirit to seal our minds and our hearts with His Word.

This seal by the Holy Spirit will protect us from deception, but this does not mean we can neglect or ignore just how powerful the deception already is. The Bible is not a crystal ball meant to be used to divine the future. This approach only ensures more deception and escapism from the coming reality. Essentially, we should hope for the best and plan for the worst. Consequently, if we are dutifully bound to tell the gospel, how are we not also bound to start talking about what is coming, especially when what is coming even requires an update to the gospel of 2000 years—"Do not take the mark of the beast!"

Consequently, we cannot keep dumbing down our congregations and protecting people from the truth of what the Bible says is coming. Instead, we must amp up the volume on our ability to destroy Satan's narrative. Besides, someone is going to be here when all of this happens. Unfortunately, no one will have much of a chance if we don't start talking about what is coming before it happens.

An Explosion of the Supernatural

Before taking on this next subject, I want to acknowledge that my intent is not to thwart the Holy Spirit in any way. I also do not want to quench our desire for the Holy Spirit in our lives, and especially its fruit or gifts. On the contrary, I believe an outpouring of the Holy Spirit is coming and that many people will be saved. However, considering the verses above, is it any wonder that signs and wonders churches are popping up all over the country?

Understanding that Satan will also have signs and wonders that will follow him right into our churches might change our ideas about the coming deception. Shockingly, it is the supernatural that may define Satan's deception. We are explicitly told in Matthew 24:24, Revelation 16:14, Revelation 13:13-14, and Revelation 19:20 that the Antichrist, demons, and other false prophets or Christ's will use their supernatural powers to convince many that they are the truth.

> *But even if an angel from Heaven or we should preach to you a gospel contrary to the one we preached to you, let him be accursed* (Galatians 1:8 NKJV).

This supernatural explosion only comes as a surprise if we have forgotten that the pagan gods of the Old Testament were false gods, but they had real demonic power. The power of these pagan gods was demonstrated in Exodus 7:11, 22, and 8:7, as well as other passages that are too numerous to count. Even though mighty Moses came to deliver Israel with signs and wonders, the Pharoah was not even phased because his wise men and magicians "did the same with their secret arts." Yet, no matter how much we are told that the supernatural world has a dark side, there is a growing obsession in the church over miracles and magic shows.

Signs and Wonders

It is as if signs and wonders are the be all and end all of Christianity. They are also creating a hierarchy among the churches and pastors. In some instances, pastors have declared themselves to be on the level of the twelve apostles. Of course, I am not trying to say that we do not need modern apostles. However, there were only twelve men that Jesus handpicked.

We also have a clear mandate not to write any more books of the Bible because there can be no new gospel. But the return of ancient spirits that were disciplined for what they did in the days of Noah is also going to cause a return of some of our spiritual weapons (1 Peter 3:1-9). Many signs and wonders will return to the church because they gave the church the victory over darkness the last time they faced off.

So, while this pouring out of the Holy Spirit may have begun, we need to be cautious because there is also a counterfeit coming. Essentially, just because there are signs and wonders does not mean that what is happening is of God. Why do I say that? Most of us know that the Bible tells us we do not need to be afraid of a prophet if his words do not come to pass. After all, a false prophet could be killed if his prophecies didn't happen. (See Deuteronomy 18:20-22.) A much less known passage is about a different kind of prophet.

If a prophet or dreamer of dreams arises among you and proclaims a sign or wonder to you, and if the sign or wonder he has spoken to you comes about, but he says, "Let us follow other gods (which you have not known) and let us worship them," you must not listen to the words of that prophet or dreamer. For the LORD your God is testing you to find out whether you love Him with all your heart and with all your soul (Deuteronomy 13:1-4 BSB).

Relationship Theology

This sends chills up my spine. I am shocked to find out that some false prophets can perform signs and wonders and rightly tell us of things that will come to pass. What I find interesting is that God allows for these fakes because He is testing us to see if we know Him or not. The idea of personally knowing God is the most important and all-encompassing paradigm of the Bible. It also parallels what I have personally found to be the most challenging passage in the Bible. Here is a quick review of Matthew 7:7-23.

The passage begins by telling us that we are God's children, and because of that, God knows how to give good gifts to those who ask, seek, and knock. Then Jesus also tells us how to give good gifts to others by living according to the Golden Rule. But one of the narratives in verse 17 that people miss is where Jesus talks about the false prophets and the wolves that stand in our way. Jesus specifically tells us that the way to recognize these false prophets or wolves is by their fruit. This part about false prophets is interesting because Jesus mentions the gifts, but then says it is the fruit that can help us sort out the wolves in the church. What comes next is the most earth-shattering verse in the Bible.

> *Not everyone who says to Me, "Lord, Lord," will enter the kingdom of Heaven, but only he who does the will of My Father in Heaven. Many will say to Me on that day, "Lord, Lord, did we not prophesy in Your name, and in Your name drive out demons and perform many miracles?" Then I will tell them plainly, "I never knew you; depart from Me, you workers of lawlessness!"* (Matthew 7:21-23 BSB)

My first reaction to this passage is, "Wow, I have never done some of these things. If these guys were fooling themselves about getting into heaven, then maybe I am fooling myself as well." Of course, this doubt subsides because the point that Jesus is trying to drive home is that He didn't know these people. They didn't have a relationship with Him. What also cannot be missed is that Jesus singled out people that were operating in the gifts of the Spirit. These same people used their gifts as a justification for why they should make it into heaven. Yet, gifts were not the most important thing, but a relationship with Jesus was.

The people who did not know Jesus were surely known for their spiritual gifts. In fact, they were probably superstars in their church. What they did not have was an intimate relationship with Jesus. Therefore, they must have been the wolves Jesus just warned us about. In other words, it looks like they were spiritually gifted people, but they also didn't have the fruit of the spirit that can only come from a deep relationship with God. This passage leads me to believe that our spiritual fruit more accurately reflects the depth of our relationship with Jesus than our gifts. Gifts have more to say about the generous nature of God because God "gives them to all men liberally" (James 5:1).

Essentially, God gives us all some kind of value, a talent, if you will, but the question becomes what we did with it. Nonetheless, it is difficult to believe any part of this story is a coincidence. Indeed, Jesus explicitly mentions three of the gifts of the Spirit (prophecy, deliverance, and miracles) that are found in 1 Corinthians 12:1-31. Jesus then says that these people were operating in these gifts without actually having a relationship with Him. This idea is beyond scary! If gifts like this started happening to me, I would probably feel like I had achieved a special connection with God. Yet, this does not appear to be the case. No matter what, all of this tells me that I have much to learn about how down-to-earth our God is.

> *But understand this: In the last days, terrible times will come. For men will be lovers of themselves, lovers of money, boastful, arrogant, abusive, disobedient to their parents, ungrateful, unholy, unloving, unforgiving, slanderous, without self-control, brutal, without love of good, traitorous, reckless, conceited, lovers of pleasure rather than lovers of God, having a form of godliness but denying its power. Turn away from such as these!* (2 Timothy 3 BSB)

The Gifts and the Giver

It is hard to say precisely when Jesus gave these gifts to these people or if they were born with them. Indeed, some people are born with unique gifts but never give God credit. What is shocking to me is that these people specifically gave Jesus credit for their gifts because they used His name, but they still didn't have a relationship with Jesus. How is this possible? Is this what Revelation 2:1-7 meant when it talks about a church that had lost its "first love"? Did these people start out loving God with all their heart and then begin to love His gifts more than they loved the Giver of the gifts?

Is this also an issue of worship? Did they begin to worship the gifts instead of God? I don't have all the answers, but we all need to ask ourselves some hard questions. Most importantly, on the day we meet Jesus, the only thing that matters is that we know Him, and He knows us. It is not going to be all about our gifts. What we did with the lives God gave us certainly will come up, but it is our relationship with Him that matters most. This same equation is found in the Lord's prayer when Jesus emphatically invited us to pray, "Thy will be done on earth as it is in heaven."

Still, how can we pray from heaven's perspective if we don't know Jesus well enough? It is knowing God, that gives us the faith and the right to pray, ask, and believe in miracles. We also have to accept God's answers and interpret them in light of the cross, which is our ultimate victory. Knowing that only God can be God will allow us to accept His answers and still keep praying earnestly for more of His will here on earth. Faith, not miracles, is the currency of heaven (Romans 4:22). Still, there is no doubt that some people have extraordinary gifts, but Christianity is not about gifts. Christianity is about having a great relationship with God.

Matthew 7, just like Deuteronomy 13, clearly shows that miracles, signs, and wonders do not always equate to a good relationship with the Giver of these same gifts. Of course, God is still going to keep on giving gifts out of His goodness. While we will need His gifts to face what is coming, we must recognize the difference between the gifts and the fruit of our "first and forever love."

Those Seeking Signs and Wonders

Unfortunately, most people aren't searching for a relationship with God. Some people even want God to prove Himself to them. But Jesus has already done that on the cross, and it changed all of history. Still, some are always searching for a sign, or are they just looking for a miracle? Indeed, sign seekers were prevalent even in Jesus' day.

Then some of the scribes and Pharisees answered, saying, "Teacher, we want to see a sign from You." But He answered and said to them, "An evil and adulterous generation seeks after a sign, and no sign will be given to it except the sign of the prophet Jonah" (Matthew 12:38-39 NKJV).

What I hear Jesus saying is that He and He alone is the sign we have been searching for. A relationship with Jesus is an everlasting gift. There is no more pain or death where Jesus is leading us to. There is only beauty beyond description and unfathomable love that awaits us there in heaven. Even the Bible asks us why do we rejoice. Do we rejoice because we have gifts? Do we rejoice because the demons are subject to us or that miracles happen when we pray? No. We rejoice because we have received some of God's grace, and because our names are written in heaven. But we don't own anything.

For who makes you so superior? What do you have that you did not receive? And if you did receive it, why do you boast as though you did not? (1 Corinthians 4:7 BSB)

Nevertheless, do not rejoice in this, that the spirits are subject to you, but rejoice that your names are written in Heaven (Luke 10:20 BSB).

Wolves Among the Sheep

What I hope most of us noticed is that the gifts of the Spirit all seem to have a purpose here on earth. My grandfather, who was a Pentecostal minister for more than 40 years, often told me that where the Pentecostal movement went wrong was when they were deciding whether the gifts of the Spirit were the churches or the individuals. Like my grandfather, F.C. Kruse, I favor the church, but I agree that certain people tend to operate better in particular gifts. However, in the final analysis, the gifts and workings of the

Spirit are God's property. Essentially, they are just different parts of the same body. Consequently, we must not come to love the gifts more than we love the Giver of the gifts.

As near as I can tell, the attitude of the "signs and wonders" churches appears to be that the greatest of those among us are the ones with the greatest gifts. This idea was in sharp contrast to what Jesus told His disciples, "If anyone desires to be first, he will be last of all and servant of all." Servanthood and the fruit of the Spirit are what allow us to sort out the wolves among the sheep. Finally, when it comes to "love, joy, peace, patience, kindness, goodness, faithfulness, gentleness, and self-control," they are going to be left wanting (Galatians 5:22-23).

What I have noticed is there is a similarity between the fruit of the Spirit and God's description of love. Still, love would never make people feel inferior just because they didn't have a particular gift. But does the Bible even say we are supposed to have all the same gifts? Paul sarcastically asks the same question found in 1 Corinthians 12:27-31, and the answer is no. While the Bible says we are to "eagerly desire the greater gifts," we forget the last part found in verse 31, "Yet I will show you a more excellent way."

The Amplified translation identifies this more excellent way as unselfish love, which happens when we use God's gifts to help other people. In this sense, seeking the gifts of the Spirit versus seeking a deeper relationship with Jesus are two different things. But how does this match the attitude of many of the mega churches or super leaders? For myself, I have questions regarding their spiritual fruit, humility, and failure to teach Bible prophecy, along with their diminishing emphasis on a deeper relationship with God.

Additionally, the diversity of gifts are not supposed to divide us; they are supposed to bring us together because they all come from the same Spirit (1 Corinthians 12:4). So why divide the church over gifts when they were explicitly given to us to encourage and sanctify the whole church? Consequently, people using the gifts to divide the church turns out to be one way we can recognize the wolves that have crept into our midst. Consequently, we must be aware that pretenders are going to enter the church even though they are operating in marvelous gifts.

Fortunately, Jesus told us, "By their fruit, you shall know them" (Matthew 7:16). We will also know them by their love for their brothers and sisters (John 13:35). These two paradigms are how we can use the Bible to discern the spirits of those presenting themselves as brothers and sisters in Christ. Lastly, if you are more interested in identifying the false prophets in the church read all of 2 Peter 2 and 2 Corinthians 11:12-15. After all, there will always be people who are masquerading as angels of light.

For we were all baptized by one Spirit to form one body—whether Jews or Gentiles, slave or free, and we were all given the one Spirit to drink (2 Corinthians 11:13 NIV).

The False Prophets Are Here

Disregard them! They are blind guides. If a blind man leads a blind man, both will fall into a pit (Matthew 15:14 BSB).

For the time will come when people will not put up with sound doctrine. Instead, to suit their desires, they will gather around them many teachers to say what their itching ears want to hear. They will turn their ears away from the truth and turn aside to myths (2 Timothy 4:3-4 NIV).

With a complete takeover of the free world imminent and the loss of ownership of our bodies, now is not the time to lack discernment over the supernatural signs and wonders that are to follow. Now is also not the time to start dumbing down the Bible or prophecy. In a strange twist, the secular world is obsessed with the supernatural, while pastors avoid it in their sermons. Now is also not the time to start blending the New Age or any other religion into Christianity. Now is the time to differentiate the worship of God in "spirit and truth" from other types of false worship or meditation.

Now is not the time to start coining new terms or coming up with new translations to fit our worldview. While I hate to single anyone out, the new "Passion" translation seems to fit the bill. Brian Simmons claims that he virtually downloaded this directly from Jesus when he was in heaven. Once there, he found a new chapter of the Bible, John 22. Thankfully, Brian has never published that book. New gospels are troublesome. When you say you are downloading the Bible, it means that this is not a translation. Instead, he is saying, "These are the literal words of Jesus."

Interestingly enough, Paul told us that even if one of the twelve apostles or an angel from heaven gave us a new gospel, "Let him be accursed" (Galatians 1:8). I could write a whole book about false prophets in the church, but I am only going to mention a couple of things because I think they are extremely dangerous. I recently listened to a Christian book called *The School of the Prophets*, which mentions that we should start talking to our own personal angels. Unfortunately, I see no biblical case for this. Furthermore, I don't believe that we need any intercessors between God and us. Intercession is the function of Jesus and the Holy Spirit. Besides, how exactly do we think these spirits about to be released from prison will present themselves to us, and what messages will they bring?

If you don't think these spirits are already contacting people as we speak, then watch *Beware of Angels* on Amazon Prime. If you are interested in some of the ways the wolves have crept into the church and begun to present a false gospel, then watch *The Submergent Church*, which is also accessible on Amazon. Since I have brought up the idea of modern prophets, I want to be clear that I do not consider myself to be a prophet or a theologian, nor am I trying to predict anything.

In fact, I hope none of what I am saying actually happens. What I have done is not prophesy. I have simply read God's Word and have tried to correlate it with "what's happening" (Luke2 21), and it has been a faith-building experience. Now more than ever, we need to cling to the Bible as our only trustworthy source of information in troubled times. Sadly, this can even lead us away from the church we are attending because they are still pretending that this isn't happening.

The Forgotten Multitude?

After this, I looked and saw a multitude too large to count, from every nation and tribe and people and tongue, standing before the throne and before the Lamb. They were wearing white robes and holding palm branches in their hands. And they cried out in a loud voice: "Salvation to our God, who sits on the throne, and to the Lamb!" (Revelations 7:9-10 BSB)

While most of the prophetic implications of this book have divided the world into two groups, there is one group of people that I have noticeably left out. I am talking about those who have not been sealed on their foreheads either way. These are the souls that have not made their choice, but soon they will be forced to go one way or the other. These are the people that I dedicate my life to helping. The "unknown multitude" are the people we need to reach with the gospel, as well as the warning not to take the MOB. Some translations say, "an innumerable multitude."

So, how can so many people get saved during the tribulation? I thought the tribulation was all about the Jews? Well, the tribulation is not about the Jews. It is about the descendents of all twelve tribes of Israel. (Read Revelation 7:1-8.) Indeed, Israel is represented by 12,000 from each of the twelve tribes of Israel or 144,000 total. This verse proves that all the promises God made to Abraham, Isaac, Jacob, and his twelve sons will be honored just like all His promises to us. But the following passage proves that God will also inherit all the nations, which is a fulfillment of Psalms 82:8. Whether these numbers for Israel are symbolic or not, it is difficult to imagine that an innumerable group of people from every tribe of the earth make it through the tribulation. But they do.

I believe their salvation will come down to the pouring out of God's Spirit, the seal on our foreheads, the revival of Bible prophecy, and the return of supernatural signs and wonders to the true church like what happened at Pentecost. One way that we can reach these people is to start talking about what will happen as soon as possible. God wants us to preach the gospel and the warning about the MOB to the ends of the earth so that more people can get saved. Lives still hang in the balance, and the church needs to heed its true purpose and wake up those who are sleeping.

The Lessor Known Gifts

When I think about the gifts presented in 1 Corinthians 12:1-31, I try and focus on the ones that will help us discern between God's angels and these escaped spirits bent on revenge. In verse 3, Paul defines what unites the church. "No one can say, 'Jesus is Lord,' except by the Holy Spirit." Then, verses 4-6 talk about "different kinds of gifts, but the same Spirit distributes them." Interestingly, these verses also seem to add some context for our spiritual gifts as if they are services or workings.

How might our dialog change if we talked more about how God has called us to serve and work in His kingdom instead of talking about how we are gifted? After all, verse 7 makes it clear that these gifts of the Spirit are "given for the common good." For our purposes, it is verses 8 and 9 that bring out some of the lesser-known gifts.

- A message of, a word of, an utterance of, or speaking with wisdom or giving wise advice

• The gift of faith

• A message of, a word of, an utterance of, or speaking with knowledge or giving correct information

Indeed, I have never met anyone who maintained that any of these gifts have ever ceased from being part of the church. Now more than ever, we need the gifts of knowledge, wisdom, and faith to discern the difference between the spirits that are coming. More importantly, the Bible is our only source of the correct information, and we will need the Holy Spirit to help us wisely divide the word of truth.

Lastly, we will need faith in God in order not to follow man. We will need encouragement to stand up and say no to the devil and his mark. We will need hope to share with a dying world. While other men's hearts will be failing them for fear, we will have a supernatural faith that says, "Henceforth there is laid up for me a crown of righteousness, which the Lord, the righteous judge, shall give me at that day: and not to me only, but unto all them also that love his appearing" (2 Timothy 4:8 KJV).

Loving the Fruit

While I enjoy the gifts that God has given to me, and I try to be open to more, the truth is that I am happier with more of the fruit of the Spirit. There honestly isn't one gift of the Spirit that I wouldn't trade for one more piece of fruit. That's not to say that I am right, but that is how I feel sometimes. Comparing fruit to gifts is much like comparing the gospel of Mary to Martha, and it is something we all need to think about. Besides, I like to remind pastors that they will be out of a job when they get to heaven.

But of course, that is probably true for all of us. Contemplating heaven is the kind of sober discussion we need to discern the truth of fruit and gifts. While I believe and support the gifts of the Spirit, I think we have to prioritize slightly here and focus on the fruit because, without them, our gifts aren't believable. After all, fruit is how we will recognize the fakes. With that in mind, here are some of my favorite sayings about the fruit of the Spirit. Please remember, I am not trying to diminish the gifts, but I am trying to keep them in perspective.

- It would appear many of the "gifts of the Spirit" aren't necessary in heaven. But the fruit of the Spirit is something we can eat every day and for all eternity.

- Fruit is delicious. Plus, it can feed us and keep us alive. All gifts are fantastic, but only a few of them can nourish our souls through a spiritual famine.

- There is a diversity of gifts, works, and service, which means (like Forest Gump's chocolates) you never know what you're going to get (1 Corinthians 12:4).

- Fruit and love typically lead to maturity, but gifts don't always equate to maturity. For example, what kind of child of God would put one of their brothers or sisters down just because they got a particular gift and their brother or sister didn't?

The Great Pouring Out of God's Spirit

With all this talk of the gifts of the Spirit, I am surprised that many have taught they have ceased. Others have even looked down upon generations of Christians for losing the gifts. Yet, one reason why we don't see the gifts of the Spirit as often as we could be is because the Holy Spirit has already put most of what we are fighting in prison. Consequently, the return of these spirits could be why the gifts are coming back in full force. We will need all of God's weapons as we fight for the minds and hearts of the innumerable multitude that God wants to reach.

With persecution on the rise, denominationalism won't matter that much longer. True churches and true believers will begin to experience prophecy, visions, dreams, wonders in heaven above, and signs in the earth beneath (Acts 2:16-21). But to pull this off and to be believable, we still need fruit to keep our feet planted on the ground. Furthermore, we must always keep our "first love" our "first love" as the world is soon to be shaken (Revelation 2:4).

The Spirit of the Lord will rest on him—the Spirit of wisdom and of understanding, the Spirit of counsel and of might, the Spirit of the knowledge and fear of the Lord, and he will delight in the fear of the Lord. He will not judge by what he sees with his eyes, or decide by what he hears with his ears (Isaiah 11:2-3 NIV).

8

The Beast Has Risen

Man Made Deception

If the "cause" is a deception, then the "cure"
is likely to be a deception.

Probably one of the things that has been rumored since the start of the false pandemic is that the Covid virus was man-made and purposely leaked. Most people haven't kept up on the testimonies given by virologists around the world, so it is really quite shocking to see what they have to say. More importantly, if this whole mess was intentionally designed and then leaked, it was an act of terrorism.

Dr. Steven Quay testified at a congressional forum about the origins of COVID-19. Dr. Quay, who is a physician and scientist, has been cited over 10,000 times. He has also invented seven different FDA medicines and holds 87 patents. What Dr. Quay clarifies is that if this virus is naturally occurring, then we should be able to find the animal of origin. Moreover, a natural infection also requires a secondary host before it can go to humans. But, once again, the secondary animal host cannot be found. This is extraordinary because the longest it has ever taken to find a natural host is three months, and the longest it has taken to find the secondary host is nine months.

After extensive testing of 1,000s of animals in China, they were not able to find any of the animal hosts. Then Dr. Quay turned his focus on what makes Covid uniquely contagious, which is its double CGG code and its Furin cleavage site. Both of these qualities make it difficult to believe that COVID-19 was of a natural origin because they are exactly what we would expect if gain of function research was being used. Dr. Quay also testifies that no Covid has had the double CGG code in over 100 years. Interestingly, we also know through Fauci's emails that he knew what they were doing with gain of function research at the Wuhan lab.

- https://www.youtube.com/watch?v=YeW5sI-R1Qg

- https://www.republicanwhip.gov/news/origins-wrap-up-the-science-points-to-a-lab-leak/

The Wuhan lab is China's only level 4 facility, so it is authorized to house dangerous biologicals like COVID-19. This kind of lab has airlocks, and everyone who goes into it has to wear special suits. Dr. Simone Gold talks about the origins of COVID-19 on her website. She also indicates that the Wuhan lab had numerous documented leaks prior to being a level 4 facility. Consequently, they should have never been given level 4 status.

- https://rumble.com/vh71ij-dr.-simone-gold-the-origins-of-covid-19-americas-frontline-doctors.html

Dr. Bret Weinstein is another evolutionary biologist and top-level scientist who is also asking, "Did Covid come from a lab?" Dr. Weinstein's conclusion was that either COVID-19 leaked from the Wuhan lab, or it was planted there to make it look like it did. Dr. Weinstein feels that this is not a normal virus. He informs us that the only labs that work on these kinds of viruses are in North Carolina and in Wuhan.

So, what does Dr. Brett think of the Covid narrative, and are we being lied to? "At a level that is it is almost impossible to fathom ... The very same people are trying to control what it is we are allowed to discuss ... They are trying to shape a narrative that even a small amount of investigation reveals is nonsense … We have to figure out how, given that all of our institutions are participants in this lie … How we can escape it with the minimal amount of damage by going around these institutions."

- https://www.youtube.com/watch?app=desktop&v=sbyIIprV9pE

- https://www.agreenroadjournal.com/2021/06/dr-robert-malone-virologist-and.html

Dr. Weinstein is also not a big proponent of the vaccine, largely because he says it doesn't act like a vaccine: First, it does not stay in the local vicinity of where it was injected. Second, the spike proteins are not supposed to leave the cells that create them, but they do. Lastly, this supposed vaccine is not biologically neutral; it is biologically active, which means it has many negative effects on different systems in our bodies. Here are some other references that indicate the cover-up of the man-made nature of COVID-19.

Rep. McCaul Calls COVID-19 Origins "Worst Cover-up in Human History"

- https://www.forbes.com/sites/jonathanpon-ciano/2021/05/30/rep-mccaul-calls-covid-19-origins-worst-coverup-in-human-history-wuhan-lab-leak-theory/?sh=1aa27e5b7277

The origin of Covid: Did people or nature open Pandora's box at Wuhan?

- https://apple.news/AXeuV0wNWQ6-TqVKcueflzw

Coronavirus Lab Leak Theory: Evidence Beyond a Reasonable Doubt

- https://www.nationalreview.com/2021/06/the-lab-leak-theory-evidence-beyond-a-reasonable-doubt/

Google Funded Virus Research by Wuhan Lab-Linked Scientist

- https://www.infowars.com/posts/google-funded-virus-research-by-wuhan-lab-linked-scientist/

An Act of Terrorism

Once we accept that the most logical origin of COVID-19 is by purposeful design, we have to accept that the whole Covid narrative is also by design. Essentially, COVID-19 is an act of terrorism. It is interesting that typically our nation does not negotiate with terrorists, but that is exactly what we are doing now. Furthermore, if this virus was man-made, but accidentally released, we would not have encountered such a massive cover-up at every level. In fact, we are not allowed to talk about any other possibilities. Censorship and boycotting of any of this information is so encompassing that it is difficult to fathom how they have even been able to do it.

The powers that be have presented a united front to the point that many of us have questioned our sanity. But if this was an act of terrorism, then why are we going along with what the terrorists want? If we would have never given in to the Taliban just because they threatened to kill .18% of Americans over 18 months, then why are we going along with this? Yet, the reason we have these amazing freedoms is because previous generations of Americans fought and died for them. Consequently, we cannot let anyone use the threat of death to take something away from us that was only made possible by the martyrdom of our founding generation.

Indeed, it has only been through the continual sacrifice of lives that we have been able to keep our freedoms. "Give me liberty, or give me death," was penned by Patrick Henry, one of the founders of America. Patrick has also said, "It is when a people forget God that tyrants forge their chains." Forgetting God and embracing lies and fear are causing a new generation to lose what has been so preciously acquired by their ancestors. But if vaccine passports become the law, then all freedoms will soon be lost. This is the kind of power no one should have, and that is especially true of Satan.

False Prophets

No one has lied to the American people more than Covid Czar Tony Fauci. With the release of his emails, we can immediately see both the dishonesty and the patronization of America. Unfortunately, only one mainstream media source mentioned any discrepancies between what Tony said in his emails versus what he said on camera or under oath. Fauci specifically lied about the possible origins of Covid because otherwise, his connections to the Wuhan lab could have made him a suspect.

Not only was Tony aware of the Wuhan's labs' gain of function research, but he was also a big supporter of developing super viruses. What kind of person thinks that is a good idea? He was also funding it through the NIH and taxpayer money. What is astonishing is that Fauci did not alert senior White House officials before lifting the ban on gain of function research in 2017. What? Our own government didn't even know gain of function research was being done in Wuhan because Fauci forgot to inform them. All of this is why Tony lied to the American government and to the American people about almost everything.

His own culpability is why Tony made up the story about how all the experts had decided that COVID-19 came from bats, when no such panel of experts did anything of the kind. These facts are why Senator/Dr. Rand Paul accused Fauci of committing perjury over his gain of function comments about the Wuhan lab. In Fauci's emails, he clearly describes gain of function research going on at Wuhan but then turns around and denies it under oath. As we have shown, the most likely source of this virus is man, and it started close to the Wuhan lab.

And the one guy connected to all of this was in charge of the investigation and the treatment plan of Covid when he had never seen one Covid patient in his life. Furthermore, Tony has never publicly admitted that natural immunity works, but he does in his emails. The reason he refuses to acknowledge natural immunity in public is because immunity would allow someone to forgo all of his restrictions and vaccines and just move on with their life. "Three Mask Tony" first tells us that masks are unnecessary, but then "adjusts" his thinking to where everyone should wear on and then three and then back to one. Even now, Tony tells us that everyone must get vaccinated, even though he admits that people with breakout infections have the same level of nasal virus whether they have been vaccinated or not.

Additionally, Dr. Simone Gold also says Dr. Fauci FOIA emails revealed: 1) He discussed gain of function research. 2) A scientist told him the virus seemed "engineered." 3) He privately admitted masks aren't effective. 4) He was aware of a possible lab leak but denied it.

What we have to realize is that after we listened to 20 months of Fauci telling us what to do, we can see that it hasn't worked because he is wrong and because he is lying. Here are a couple of other sources to understand why we should do the opposite of what Fauci says.

- https://www.breitbart.com/politics/2021/05/25/sen-paul-fauci-committed-perjury-over-gain-of-function-comments-related-to-wuhan-lab/

- https://townhall.com/tipsheet/katiepavlich/2021/05/11/rand-paufauci-n2589260

- https://www.dailywire.com/news/fauci-didnt-alert-white-house-when-gain-of-function-research-ban-lifted-said-worth-pandemic-risk-in-2012-report?itm_source=parsely-api&utm_source=cnemail&utm_medium=email

- https://www.foxnews.com/opinion/tucker-carlson-is-dr-fauci-under-criminal-investigation

- https://www.extremelyamerican.com/post/dr-fauci-funder-and-founder-of-the-covid-19-crime-against-humanity

Mystery Babylon and Pharmakeía

And never again will the light of a lamp shine in you, and never again will the voice of the bridegroom and bride be heard in you; for your merchants were the great [powerful] *and prominent men of the earth* [princes, rulers, important people] *because all the nations were deceived and misled by your sorcery* [witchcraft, your magic spells, and poisonous charms] (Revelation 18:23).

I realize that many people are struggling with all of this because, so far, this sounds like a grand conspiracy that is impossible to believe. So, hear me out. What I want to address is that there are only two ways anything happens. Either someone plans it, or it's an accident. Reading about the origins of our faith, the one thing we must recognize is that everything started when Satan conspired against God. Therefore, every Christian should be looking for signs of Satan's conspiracy in our own lives. However, during the end times, God has not left a lot to chance. God specifically tells us who, what, and how this conspiracy is going to be perpetrated upon us.

While I have covered this passage in my "Mystery Babylon" series, a pastor friend had to remind me about it. The context of the verse above is talking about "Mystery Babylon," which is identified as the perpetrator for much of the deception that is coming. This same cabal goes back to the Tower of Babel, which was the birthplace of Babylon. For our purposes, Mystery Babylon also has connections to the Divided Kingdom of Daniel and the "Beast" government of Revelation. What follows gives us some additional clues as to how this all comes together.

When it says, "Never again will the light of a lamp shine in you, and never again will the voice of the bridegroom and bride be heard in you," I believe he is talking about the end of our relationship with God. After all, God is a "lamp unto our feet, and a light unto our path." Jesus has also said to us that He is the light of the world. Additionally, it cannot be doubted that Jesus is indeed the Bridegroom and that we are His bride. What is disturbing is that suddenly the bride and groom can never speak again. Revelation 18:23 is a perfect, and yet tragic, rendering of someone who is lost with no further hope of salvation.

What else could do that? We have to assume they have probably taken the MOB. We assume this because there has never been anything until now that has been able to sever our relationship with Jesus. Then comes the trillion-dollar question: "Exactly who are these people that are going to do this to us?" Well, obviously, some parts of Mystery Babylon will remain a mystery, but this verse clearly tells us that some of the people are the "great and prominent men of the earth." Not only are they powerful, but they are rulers, princes, and famous people. Yet, one of the parts most people miss is about how they are wealthy merchants.

These wealthy international merchants, companies, businesses, and corporations form what amounts to a cabal. Like the 62 rich men we keep mentioning, they own all the key players needed to pull something like this off. The mistake most people make is that they think this is all political, but the people who are pulling this stuff off own both political parties in the world's biggest case of good cop, bad cop.

Government of Norway Indicted for Crimes Against Humanity Over "Planned False Pandemic"

- https://www.thelibertybeacon.com/govt-of-norway-indicted-for-crimes-against-humanity-over-planned-false-pandemic/?fbclid=IwAR3qkT6Ld-RQBZdnRU0yFhH8n VKDDFlKcl6aU23zycLFt_nVJSjUNzII2zs

Global Conspiracy

Revelation 18:23 gives us the last piece of the puzzle about how these people pull off the impossible. What exactly, besides the MOB, could ruin our relationship with God? It says, "Because all the nations were deceived and misled by your sorcery" (witchcraft, your magic spells, and poisonous charms). But even this is an inadequate translation. The Greek word *pharmakeía* (5331) means to administer/use drugs or medicine; drug-related sorcery or spells, which is certainly a good description of a vaccine. Hopefully, something inside us will wake up when I say that Pharmakeía is our word for pharmacy.

So, let me get this straight. Something is being plotted by Mystery Babylon that will cause the light to go out in us so that we can never hear the words of the Bridegroom again. The people who will perpetrate this conspiracy against us will be wealthy merchants, great leaders, and famous people. They will trick and deceive us through something that we can find at the pharmacy or in our doctor's office. (If you don't have chills right now, then I think you better read this section again.) Now remember I have been teaching this for 10+ years.

Another thing Revelation 18:23 directly addresses is the idea that we can be tricked into taking a drug, vaccine, or medication from our pharmacy that could end the Bridegroom's voice inside us. There are many false teachers out there who are teaching there can be no deception surrounding the MOB. But this verse appears to contradict that idea. Even the word "Covid" (Certificate of Vaccination ID) tells us what the real agenda is, and nanotechnology is more than up to fulfilling the task. Indeed, biometric nanotechnology can identify and upload everything about us to an artificial intelligence. From its inception to its name, Covid has been designed to herd us into the paddocks they have already prepared for us. Just like our elections, suddenly merchants, professional associations, companies, businesses, and corporations are all in on the deception.

Unfortunately, most people don't know that there is already an old law on the books that says our government has the right to make us take a vaccine. Apparently, this goes back to the Supreme Court case of Jacobson v. Massachusetts in 1905, over the right not to take the smallpox vaccine. None of this is a coincidence. In fact, if the international merchants were not in on the deal, then how could they be able to keep us from buying, selling, or getting a job? Just look around and see the way the Covid narrative is being used to give birth to beastly controls. This cabal or New World Order has been making plans and checking them twice. Make sure to read the quote below, because false pandemics have always been part of the plan.

Pope Francis calls for "global governance and universal vaccines."

- https://www.lifesitenews.com/news/pope-francis-calls-for-global-governance-and-universal-vaccines-in-letter-to-globalist-financial-summit

Exclusive: Former Pfizer VP to AFLDS: "Entirely possible this will be used for massive-scale depopulation."

- https://www.americasfrontlinedoctors.com/exclusive-former-pfizer-vp-to-aflds-entirely-possible-this-will-be-used-for-massive-scale-depopulation/

Feds say employers can require vaccines and offer incentives

- https://www.axios.com/employers-coronavirus-covid-vaccine-require-incentives-e8f5426e-62c5-40cd-9075-86fe72e8dc84.html

Houston Methodist hospital able to require COVID-19 vaccines.

- https://www.washingtonpost.com/nation/2021/06/13/methodist-vaccine-lawsuit-dismissed/

- https://abcnews.go.com/US/117-employees-sue-houston-methodist-hospital-requiring-covid/story?id=77977011

Quote from Jacques Attali, 1981, advisor to François Mitterrand

The future will be about finding a way to reduce the population. We start with the old, because as soon as they exceed 60-65 years, people live longer than they produce and that costs society dearly. Then the weak, then the useless that do not help society because there will always be more of them, and above all, ultimately, the stupid. Euthanasia will have to be an essential tool in our future societies, in all cases. Of course, we will not be able to execute people or build camps. We get rid of them by making them believe that it is for their own good. Overpopulation, and mostly useless, is something that is too costly economically. Socially, too, it is much better when the human-machine comes to an abrupt standstill than when it gradually deteriorates. Neither will we be able to test millions upon millions of people for their intelligence, you bet that! We will find or cause something a pandemic targeting certain people, a real economic crisis or not, a virus affecting the old or the fat, it doesn't matter, the weak will succumb to it, the fearful and stupid will believe in it and seek treatment. We will have made sure that treatment is in place, treatment that will be the solution. The selection of idiots then takes care of itself: You go to the slaughter by yourself. ["The Future of Life" - Jacques Attali, 1981] Interviews with Michel Salomon, Les Visages de l'avenir collection, editions Seghers.

Interesting Note: Will Kamala Harris Fulfill this 1933 Vision and Prophecy | Perry Stone

This video covers an end-times prophecy by William Branham about a woman who would become president, which occurs after a president steps down. The video also talked about how the world would see the coming of a new "ism." Could this be referring to transhumanism?

- https://www.youtube.com/watch?v=zYkmlXqAuv M&feature=youtu.be

No More Slow Decay

I used to think that the end would be some kind of slow decay. After all, if a frog jumps into hot water, the frog jumps right out. But now I have concluded, there is nowhere in the world for the frog to jump. The global cabal is in control, and they are breaking all the rules and disregarding our Constitution. Meanwhile, every institution that God has set up has now fallen, shut down, or is illegal. It is hate speech to believe anything that God says.

Yet, the Bible predicted all of this. Who else but God could have known that one day a simple mark could identify someone and provide all the details of their life? How could this same mark verify how much money someone had? The MOB is the perfect example of how prophecy is so powerful. God cannot be fooled or outsmarted, and prophecy is the calling card of God because He owns the future. Prophecy also proves that God is the real author of human history. For example, most people do not know that Jesus fulfilled more than 300 prophecies that prove beyond a shadow of a doubt that Jesus was the Messiah.

• https://www.clintbyars.com/blog/2020/7/20/jesus-fulfilled-over-300-prophecies

But the real question before us is why are there eight times as many prophecies about the second coming of Jesus than the first coming? Because the deception that is coming is just that good. Unfortunately, a warning won't be helpful if no one is sharing what the Bible says is to come. The warnings of prophecy are why Jesus stood outside Jerusalem and wept because the people could not discern the time of their visitation (Luke 19:44). I believe that Jesus is weeping right now and for the same reasons, some of which are still surrounding Jerusalem. Unfortunately, most Christians have not embraced the "miracle of Israel," which is why I recommend either movie by the same name.

However, the best book I have ever read on Israel or the fulfilment of Bible prophecy is Jonathan Cahn's *The Oracle.* We are all living in the days of miracles because what the Bible says was going to happen is happening right now. Unfortunately, there is no standing up or encouraging us that Jesus is coming soon. Consequently, if this book does nothing more than get people to start talking about what is in their Bibles, then it has been a success.

The Warning of Prophecy

Woe unto them that call evil good, and good evil; that put darkness for light, and light for darkness; that put bitter for sweet, and sweet for bitter! Woe unto them that are wise in their own eyes and prudent in their own sight! (Isaiah 5:20-21 KJV)

While we Christians have reasons to stand up and lift up our heads, those without faith will not be experiencing the same thing. For them, now begins a time of woes. The Harbingers are not just of America's destruction but of the coming beast system now in full view. The "powers and principalities" are in complete control of everything in the world, and that is why, for a time, they will prevail against the saints (Revelation 13:7). Of course, I had hoped for America, but it appears that Mystery Babylon is in complete control of us and the world. But it is never over until it is over, and the sheep have not yet been separated from the goats. Until then, we are called to redeem all that we can.

We are called to be salt in light of this decay. We need to look to the Spirit of God in us to arise and walk before a world that still needs Jesus. When the book, *The Harbinger,* first came out around 9/11, people repented. Yet, few have read the second more recent book, and even fewer showed up for *The Return* that Jonathan Cahn organized in Washington D.C. Instead, all of it was buried beneath the headlines of 2020. While I have no hope that things will go back to normal, I do have hope of the soon return of Jesus. I also believe God will sustain us through the trials that are coming so that we can be a witness to God's glory.

Yet, the chilling reality is that America has ceased to be good. Even more shocking is that the church has failed to recognize our enemy. Much of this is because we have stopped reading the prophetic parts of our Bibles. Instead, we have willingly fallen for deception and even shut our doors. Unfortunately, the implosion of America looms like nothing before. Our national debt alone tells the story of a nation that cannot pay its bills but is willing to borrow more money just to pretend for a little while longer.

9

The Beast Is Evolving

Proof Versus Probability

I started pre-med back in 1986, and that required that I take all of the core sciences. Evolution was the dominant theory, and so I loved to debate people about it. It is hard to understand how I can remember something so unrelated 35 years later. Yet, in one of my biology classes, I remember the professor talking about how strange viruses are. The question was how evolution could have produced them because they are not even alive. Adaptation, the driving force of evolution, in no way made them more likely to survive.

Then the professor said, "It is almost as if they were designed to carry a genetic payload to every cell of our body." Fast forward 20 years, and I would realize that the convergence of transhumanism, viruses, and the vaccine narrative would probably give us the MOB scenario. But the one thing I could never understand is how they would be able to push a genetic payload into every cell of our body. Yet, while doing some basic search on the connection between magnetic technologies and genetic therapies, I nearly fell out of my chair.

I was shocked to find a plethora of magnetic nanotechnology readily available to promote the distribution of genetic components throughout the body. These technologies would make the Covid jab 1000s of times more effective by dispersing its effects throughout the body. Curiously, some people are even demonstrating that their vaccination sites are magnetic for a period of time. Now ask yourself a few questions. First, when was the last time people spent a lot of time and money developing something that they were not going to use? Second, why would so many competing companies be trying to figure out how to push genetic components throughout our bodies if they weren't trying to change our DNA?

The Beast and the Vaccine

Why are all of the genetic therapies and biometric tracking nanotechnologies always paired with vaccines? The answer becomes obvious—they are going to use the vaccine narrative to establish their real goals. Because the vaccine narrative gives them access to our bodies and is paired with all the technologies that fit the connotations of the real MOB, now is the time to sound the alarm. The only question I have is whether they have the genetic codes they want to push. Here are some links that talk about why magnetic therapy could be a part of these vaccines. I also included some technologies that can be used to transfect cells, and guide or push biological agents throughout the body including: superparamagnetic nanotechnologies, magnetofection, and SPIONS, which are linked to "mad cow disease."

- https://www.bitchute.com/video/t5Sjxajd2E13/

- https://pubmed.ncbi.nlm.nih.gov/24715289/

- https://www.redvoicemedia.com/2021/06/exposed-magnetism-intentionally-added-to-vaccine-to-force-mrna-through-entire-body/

- https://www.scientistlive.com/content/new-magnetic-technology-launched

- https://realcoronanews.com/2020/05/14/luciferase-enzyme-makes-implantable-quantum-dot-microneedle-vaccine-work/

- https://pubs.acs.org/doi/pdf/10.1021/jacs.7b06022

- https://www.sciencedirect.com/topics/medicine-and-dentistry/superparamagnetic-iron-oxide-nanoparticle

The fact remains, there is technology available that could make this vaccine the MOB. However, we have already shared how this vaccine has been called an operating system. We have also been told by Tal Zaks that they are messing with the "software of life." While I can't prove just what kind of operating system this is, I am unwilling to take the chance. However, many forms of nanotechnology could also fit this description of being an operating system.

- https://stateofthenation.co/?p=46766

Most Christians have never put together the idea that Satan needs access to our bodies to execute his greatest conspiracy, which was also true of his first temptation. Indeed, to think that Satan would never be able to come up with another forbidden fruit would be a mistake. Even now, the Covid lie has provided Satan what he has always wanted—access to the temple of God. But if there is nothing going on here in 2021, then why is everyone in the world pushing an emergency use only not-a-vaccine if there is no emergency?

Why, if the vaccine is so safe and works so well, are governments having to force everyone in the medical field to take them? Why doesn't the world find this fact troubling? How can we not see the hypocrisy of saying that the people who have been trained and certified to make our medical decisions are suddenly not capable of making their own?

- https://www.infowars.com/posts/sunday-live-military-purging-dissidents-who-speak-out-against-marxist-critical-race-theory/

Sins Against the Body

We are losing our freedoms concerning our body, and very few are sounding the alarm. Now for the record, I hope that I am wrong about the genetic manipulation by these supposed vaccines. Yet, the genetic connection is crucial to be able to see the broader possibilities regarding the MOB. Unfortunately, most people believe their bodies are nothing more than a box we live in. But this is not true.

Our bodies are a temple that is specific to our spirit and the Holy Spirit. Our earthly and future heavenly bodies are a part of our eternal and unique identity. The temple idea is why we teach people to honor their bodies and not defile them. Unfortunately, some sins connect our bodies and our souls. Read all of 1 Corinthians 3:16-23, but verses 18 and 20 specifically highlight the idea of sinning against our own body. In verse 15, it talks about what we unite our bodies to (as in a prostitute), we link to Christ.

This passage makes the case that our body is connected to our Spirit and the Holy Spirit. God cannot become one flesh with us if we have become one flesh with a demon. However, when we think about our bodies as boxes, we are dismissing part of our triune nature. That is like rejecting the triune nature of God. In that analogy, Jesus was the physical body of God (Colossians 2:9).

Ignoring the Genetic Narrative

At this point, many of us may still fail to see the connections of transhumanism or genetic manipulation in the Bible, and I understand completely because it all sounds like a fairy tale. But if we are going to dismiss this genetic narrative in the Bible, then here is a list of what we must abandon.

1. We have to ignore or spiritualize the idea that Satan can have offspring or children.

2. We have to spiritualize the Nephilim and the giants and ignore their physical differences, which would indicate they had different DNA.

3. We have to ignore a clear warning not to mix species or "kinds" in the Bible (Leviticus 19:19). Why would God warn us of something that has only recently become possible?

4. We have to assume that our very conscience and our nature have nothing to do with our DNA. We also have to ignore the evidence that this is what happens when we transfer DNA from one creature to another.

5. We have to ignore the fact that our new body will look exactly like this one and that we will be recognizable to our family and friends for all eternity. If we change our DNA too much, this wouldn't be possible.

6. We have to ignore the fact that God wrote our DNA and hypothesize that changing our DNA would not change our identity.

7. We also have to reason away why God made numerous natural barriers that make it impossible for us to change our DNA. We also have to ignore God's commands for everything to only reproduce after its kind.

8. We have to assume that there are no sins that affect our body.

While I have made my case, I hope that I am wrong. But whether I am wrong or right, there is a choice that is coming. We are going to have to decide if we are keeping our original genetic material or not, and this is part of the issue with this supposed vaccine. While there have been many controversial points, many people can see the logic that it is a bad idea to change anything that God did. Since most people would agree that God wrote our DNA, it seems it should be a bad idea to modify or tamper with our genetic material. Again, Francis Fukuyama, a Nobel peace prize-winning scientist, called this "The World's Most Dangerous Idea."

Can Genetic Markers Be the MOB?

Does a genetic marker fulfill the idea of the MOB? For example, could a genetic marker be considered any of the following: a stamp, etching, sculpture, seal, imprint, signet, brand with a die, or engraving that "provides undeniable identification," a symbol showing an irrefutable connection between the two parties, an identification-marker, an owner's unique "brand or mark"?

Do we use genetic markers to define ownership, brand, or determine rights of creation? The answer to many of these issues is yes. Already we have the testimony of Tal Zaks saying that, "The individual or subject is no longer a creation of God but a creation of man, meaning the individual or subject could be the object of a 'patent.'"

- https://thewashingtonstandard.com/bombshell-moderna-chief-medical-officer-admits-mrna-alters-dna/

What is a patent? According to *Webster's Dictionary*, a patent can be about the exclusive control and possession of a particular individual or party; protected by a trademark or a brand name to establish proprietary or property rights analogous to what is conveyed by letters (of patent). A patent can also invoke the right to exclude others from making, using, or selling an invention, which gives them a monopoly or right so granted.

It is clear that from the perspective of Mr. Zaks, those genetic codes are indeed patentable because they invented them. When someone takes these codes, they become altered genetically. Essentially, they have overwritten their God-given mRNA codes. Changing one line of code is all that is needed to create an argument for a patent. The code itself also implies ownership and branding. It also "provides undeniable identification, shows an irrefutable connection between the two parties, and exhibits an owner's unique brand-mark."

Companies like Monsanto have been patenting work based on the same premise. They take something God made and then change a few codes to claim it as their creation. The other obvious correlation with how our DNA connects and unmistakably links us together is our familial relationships. Without these familial codes, parents have no legal rights to the children. This argument is being made right here on earth. Why can't it be made in heaven? Only God can know and decide.

Can Someone's DNA Keep Them from Being Saved?

Yes. Enter the Nephilim narrative. Potentially, those who take the MOB could be like the Nephilim, who were human hybrids, and they could not be saved. Moreover, they were un-redeemable because they were never God's children. He didn't create them, but Satan did. Consequently, they were created in Satan's image, which is why the first versions of the Nephilim didn't look like us or Jesus. Again, our DNA is what determines our image and makes God's children look like Him. We cannot be God's imagers if we change our DNA.

Remember, God never created the Nephilim, nor did He ever call them good. In fact, the word Nephilim means "fallen ones." They were also traditionally referred to as "soulless ones." Not only did God send the flood to destroy the Nephilim, but God also ordered the second wave of them to be killed everywhere they were found. One of the possible implications of this ethnic cleansing was to keep the bloodlines pure, but especially those of the Messiah. Specifically, the descendants of Israel, Esau, Lot, and the Philistines were all commanded by God to rid their lands of the Nephilim. (See: Gen 14:5-6, Numbers 13:32-33, Deuteronomy 1:26-28, 2:10-11, 2:2-23, 3:11; 1 Samuel 17 and 2 Samuel 21:15-22.)

Here's my thought. What if Satan has finally come up with a way to change our genes to be more like the Nephilim? That would be quite the deception, wouldn't it? It would explain why someone has to choose to change their DNA, or it wouldn't hold up in the court of heaven. Unfortunately, the reality is that we can change our genetic material, and this supposed vaccine is only the warm-up. The question now becomes, how much genetic change is too much?

The Unsavable Sin

What cannot be escaped is that if we talked about changing something else God wrote, such as the Bible, most people would certainly see that as a catastrophic problem. Another hole in our understanding is why I have never seen one explanation for why we can't be saved after taking the MOB that made any sense. Instead, many people are focused on the idea of worship. However, I have heard many testimonies of people who have worshiped demons and later became Christians.

Even the idea of a chip or some kind of intricate tattoo could easily fit this description, but the problem is they are both so easily removed. The MOB, like the genetic components of this vaccine, can't be removed or changed. When we cannot repent of some-thing, that is the equivalent of a seared conscience, a reprobate mind, or even blaspheming the Holy Spirit. If the MOB were just worship, then Satan would have used it before. No. The MOB must be something new—a choice we have never had before.

At the very least, the MOB would have to be a new form of worship or a revival of an old form of worship. It is also likely to have something to do with the Days of Noah. Both of these ideas are somewhat satisfied by the genetic manipulation narrative. Not surprisingly, most people fail to understand that DNA forms the construct and parameters of our minds, as well as our fundamental nature. Not only could we be changing intricate memories, thoughts, and behavioral patterns, but we may be opening up our "third eye."

Furthermore, very few people have come to grips with the idea that DNA is one of the languages of God. When God speaks, it changes reality, which is why He never changes. If He did, God wouldn't be as good as He is right now because God is already perfect. The problem is that if we alter or revoke what God wrote in our DNA, then it could change the reality of who we are.

So why is God allowing this to happen? I believe God allows it because love requires choices and freedoms. Yet, even heaven has rules that govern creators and their creations. So, if arguments of ownership and patent can be made here on earth, why not heaven? If genetic differences provide a legal obstacle to their children, then why doesn't this apply in the heavenly courts? Still, none of this matters because all five parts of the MOB scenario are happening right now.

If we allow our world governments to set up beastly systems, then we are allowing ourselves to be marked and controlled in the future. This scenario is why I am not saying this is the MOB or that I even know what the MOB is. I am saying that this fits the minimum requirements for the MOB scenario. Boom.

The failure to disclose the ingredients or submit these supposed vaccines to independent testing breaks all the rules of medicine and requires trust I do not have. The vaccine passports and the available beastly nanotechnologies are more than enough to make my MOB radar go off relentlessly. Consequently, if there is one thing that Christians should agree on, it is that no one can have these kinds of powers over us.

Yet, the church isn't saying anything, which is why a simple chiropractor is looking for any way he can to sound the alarm. Having the right to deny access to our bodies is the only way we can be sure that we never take the MOB, and so we know that is what Satan is ultimately after. Satan wants to defile our temple.

The Nephilim Mind

Have you ever thought about how in the days of Noah it was somehow possible that "every intent of the thought of (their) heart was only evil continually." Yet, the Bible teaches that we have a dual nature. While our flesh serves the law of sin, in our minds we serve Christ (Romans 7:25). Nephilim didn't have this dual nature because they served the law of sin in their minds and bodies. Could this have something to do with the genetic manipulation that was done to them?

I think we have to consider there is a strong possibility that changing our genetic material could produce a seared conscience, which could be why the Nephilim were truly unredeemable. Could a different mind-set also explain why they had a natural enmity with God and His children? Indeed, it becomes obvious that the age-old "War of the Seeds" has something to do with the fact that different seeds made each of them different. So, unless we are willing to throw out the Nephilim narrative of the Bible, we must face the fact that they had different DNA. Likewise, these genetic changes could be why the Nephilim had reprobate minds.

The Nephilim and the MOB

• They are both connected to the days of Noah.

• They both defy God and worship Satan.

- They are at odds with God's people.

- Neither of them can be saved.

- Since the Nephilim probably had different DNA, could this mean that the MOB changes our genetic components?

The Choice to Stay Human

No one can serve two masters. Either you will hate the one and love the other, or you will be devoted to the one and despise the other (Matthew 6:24 NIV).

None of the theology surrounding Genesis 6 or the Nephilim narrative ultimately matter unless they are happening again. Unfortunately, a genetic revolution is upon us, and like it or not, we will all have to make a choice. Sadly, the church is unaware of the World's Most Dangerous Idea. Even more importantly, an entirely new generation has so forgotten what was in their Bibles that they didn't even recognize when it was happening again.

We are coming to a turning point in human history. The "times of the Gentiles" appears to be coming to a close. I say this because the blood of Jesus cannot redeem those whom the beast has marked. Essentially, we could be entering a new dispensation or covenant. The MOB itself may also represent a re-enactment of some form of Old Testament law. While I am not saying the age of grace is over, there does seem to be a new limit to how far grace can go.

Knowing these changes and remembering that "people perish for lack of knowledge" means that we must begin to speak out about this new deception of Pharmakeía, which are drugs, medicine, vaccines, genetic therapy, and witchcraft. Essentially, Satan has come to tempt us with another piece of forbidden fruit that we must take into our bodies. However, there is one question that I cannot answer, and it keeps me awake during the day.

Exactly how much can I change my DNA and still be related

to Jesus? How much can I change my DNA until I am no longer considered a human being instead of some other kind of being? This question has no answer. So, we must err on the side of caution. This is why we must resist the Covid narrative and deny the access to our bodies that they so desire.

The Great Division Is Happening

And whereas thou saw iron mixed with miry clay, they shall mingle themselves with the seed of men: but they shall not cleave one to another, even as iron is not mixed with clay (Daniel 2:43 KJV).

While it is becoming obvious that this supposed vaccine has become the dividing point of the whole world, the Bible said this would happen. Everywhere people are unfriending their families and even long-time friends over the Covid narrative. Consequently, this verse is being fulfilled as we speak, but no one is talking about it. There really are people with mingled seed and some without it entirely. Once again, an age-old "enmity" has been awakened.

Already, the natural health world is in an uproar and wants to keep vaccinated people away from them over the ideas of shedding and infertility. Meanwhile, the vaccinated are blaming the fact that the vaccine doesn't work and the new variants on the unvaccinated. It is the vaccinated that approve of vaccine passports that would put everyone who doesn't take the vaccine in a concentration camp. After all, most people can't live without one paycheck.

Yet, "United We Stand, and Divided We Fall" is still the equation for the survival of every country. Creating division is how they formed communism and why the communists said they would destroy America without firing a shot. They aren't doing that bad, are they? Indeed, the pandemic is all about dividing us and destroying our financial resources so that we can hate each other. After all, hate is what hell is built upon.

10

What Can We Do?

Crickets in the Pulpit

Let the pulpit resound with the doctrines and sentiments of religious liberty. Let us hear the dangers of thralldom to our consciences from ignorance, extreme poverty, and dependence; in short, from civil and political slavery. Let us see delineated before us the true map of man.

—*John Adams*

Can you imagine going somewhere for the past year and a half where many people gather to hear different speakers, hang out, connect, and supposedly be honest? But the curious thing is that not one time did anyone there ever bring up COVID-19, wearing masks, being shut down, mail-in ballots, vaccines, genetic therapy, or vaccine passports. Well, I can. For most of us, that would be our church. Indeed, half the time, I am asking myself, "What planet are they living on?"

We also need to realize that silence is acquiescence. Maybe they are being silent because none of this is a problem from their perspective. These topics have been virtually the only things people want to talk about for a year and a half, and yet, the churches completely ignore it as if our Bibles have nothing to say. But this is not the separation of church and state; it is the separation of church from reality. If this doesn't change, the church will soon become irrelevant because it ignores what is happening right in front of our eyes.

Even more importantly, what is happening is truly troubling for all of us, but the church is still ignoring it. Of course, there are several things that I think are contributing to the church's silence. The first is that the church has never been more divided than it is right now. The second is that people are being protected from what the Bible says because of political correctness. Ministers know that people are divided over these issues, so they avoid them. Can't blame them there.

But can we allow the church to become afraid of the truth just because it will offend many? Can we sacrifice truth so that more people stay and keep tithing? Unfortunately, the church has become especially afraid of political narratives, even though politics are what killed Jesus. Ultimately, nowhere does the Bible teach separation of church and state. Yet, this silence is eerily similar to what Hitler did to the churches right before he took control. Hitler was able to silence the church and turn one group of people into scapegoats, and this is how the "great holocaust" happened.

No Fellowship with Lies

Of all the problems I have with the church these days, the most significant one is they going along with known lies, as they ignore what is clearly in God's Word about the end times. If Jesus is "the way, the truth, and the life," then how can we go along with a lie in any area? This is especially true when this same lie is how the "beast government" sets up the trap that will ensnare Christians and close our churches. From my perspective, here are some of the worst lies about the Covid narrative.

1. The first lie is that ordinary healthy people die of Covid. But this is entirely wrong, as we have addressed. If we are under 65 and have no underlying conditions, we have vir-

tually zero chance of dying from Covid. So, why would we wear a mask, close our business, lose everything we have, or take an experimental vaccine?

2. It is a lie that there are no other suitable forms of treatment for Covid except a vaccine. Even Fauci knew that hydroxy-chloroquine was a potent inhibitor of other SARS/coronavirus infections. But because of a study by the *Lancet*, they could remove a 60-year-old effective treatment based on a smear campaign by the most reputable scientific journal. It is extremely rare for the *Lancet* to retract an article, but the damage has been done. The same thing has happened to Ivermectin, which we have even given to our troops before going overseas.

• https://virologyj.biomedcentral.com/articles/-10.1186/1743-422X-2-69

• https://americanideals.info/american-journal-of-medicine--admits-hcq-works-to-treat-covid-19/

3. The third lie is in the number of Covid deaths themselves. You cannot change the rules for how death certificates are done at the beginning of a pandemic; otherwise, it cannot be compared. A guidance change by the CDC allowed for suspicion alone to determine the cause of death. The second guidance change allowed an "active" or immediate condition to supersede the normal procedure of using the "underlying condition" as the cause of death. Furthermore, these changes were incentivized when health insurance companies began paying more money for Covid diagnosis and treatment. The CDC director specifically admitted that financial incentives were inflating the numbers. (See previous reference.)

4. Then we have the mask mandate. The lie here is that these masks can only filter something that is 800 times larger than Covid. Furthermore, when the British Medical Journal did a systematic review of over 31 mask studies, they did not find any statistical difference between the people that wore a mask and those who did not. (See previous ref.)

5. The fifth lie is that this vaccine is not a vaccine; it is genetic therapy. There is no Covid virus inside this vaccine. Instead, they use their own specifically coded mRNA to override our God-given RNA to make us manufacture something similar to a spike protein. This spike pathogen makes us sick and causes more complications than any vaccine in history.

6. The sixth lie is we can go back to normal if we take this vaccine. Now both Fauci and Walensky have even admitted that the vaccine doesn't work because it allows for infection and transmission of the virus.

7. The seventh lie is that Covid makes us sick, but the vaccine doesn't. Unfortunately, more people get sick from the supposed vaccine than from Covid. Remember, 80% of people testing positive for Covid are asymptomatic, while 50-80% of the vaccinated get sick.

8. If 70% of adults in America are vaccinated, how can the Covid infections keep going up? This is also what happened in Chile.

- https://www.forbes.com/sites/joewalsh/2021/04/06/covid-is-surging-in-chile-despite-high-vaccination-rates—-heres-why-the-us-should-take-notice/?sh=1906df49b6c7

9. The ninth lie is that these vaccines are safe. Recall our coverage of the VAERS statistics with 19,000+ people dead. But the main point is that if someone is not at risk of

dying from Covid, then there is no reason for them to be forced to take medical treatment or do anything differently. Meanwhile, half of the vaccines have already been pulled in the first few months. In Europe, almost 5400 people are dead, and nearly 240,000 injured from vaccines.

- https://medicalkidnap.com/2021/04/09/5365-dead-238949-injuries-european-database-of-adverse-drug-reactions-for-covid-19-vaccines/

- https://www.cbsnews.com/news/astrazeneca-covid-vaccine-europe-countries-suspend-blood-clot-worries/

- https://news.yahoo.com/j-j-vaccine-placed-hold-164504729.html

- https://www.openvaers.com

10. The tenth lie has to do with accepting vaccines in general without ever asking what is in them or how they were developed to ensure no moral dilemmas are present. Virtually all vaccines have an animal substrate to stabilize the active ingredient. How is this not mixing species? Nearly all human vaccines are either developed with fetal tissue or use fetal lines to test the vaccine. How is this not benefiting from abortion?

11. If natural immunity is 80% at curing Covid with no symptoms at all (assuming the test actually works), and the immunity to Covid lasts for decades, then why would I take an experimental vaccine? These vaccines don't work, and now people already need boosters just to protect themselves.

Coronavirus Immunity May Last Years, Possibly Even Decades

- https://www.forbes.com/sites/tommybeer/2020/11/17/coronavirus-immunity-may-last-years-possibly-even-decades-study-suggests/?sh=425b90634185

The Blind Leading the Blind

Meanwhile, we have Franklin Graham (whom I love and support), telling us that taking a vaccine is what Jesus would do, and he is not the only one. I really couldn't believe it! How could he possibly know what Jesus would do in this situation? More importantly, why would Jesus need a vaccine? Why would Jesus be afraid of Covid? Why would Jesus participate in all these lies? Is Jesus Mr. Rogers, or is Jesus the One who bore the sins of the whole world when He could have just ignored them?

- https://www.chvnradio.com/articles/franklin-graham-supports-vaccines-and-says-jesus-would-too

What is so dangerous is that when someone tells us what Jesus would do, they are speaking for God, which means they are declaring themselves to be a prophet of God. This kind of thinking is how the Covid narrative has shut the churches down with virtually no protest. For example, Andy Stanley (another pastor I love) says he is embarrassed by churches that wouldn't shut down. While I agree we need to get more creative, I was embarrassed that he can't discern what time it is. But look at where we are. Are our pastors really going to say nothing? People are losing the freedom of their own body and losing jobs in the process. They are destroying our whole society and taking our freedom. Would Jesus really go along with that? Would Jesus submit or give in to lies? It's your turn to answer.

The Christian Dilemma

I get that we are called to be peacemakers, but how exactly can we keep the peace and still be on the side of truth? If the church does not begin to address what the media is saying or what's on television, soon we will become both irrelevant and lukewarm. The idea that Christians are neutral even in the political realm is going to be an impossibility. Pastors and patrons around the world are being arrested for Covid violations. Free speech is gone. We must not let that happen. Like any situation, discernment is the key to knowing when to resist and when to give in.

The issue is motive. Love and hate have different motives. Along this line of reasoning, "If someone's mask works, then why do I have to wear one? If someone's vaccine works, then why do I have to take it?" But hate doesn't allow for choices or even a discussion about masks or mandates, which is why none of this is about saving lives. The mandates are about control and manipulation. Remember the famous quote of Lord Acton, "Power tends to corrupt and absolute power corrupts absolutely." That is why we cannot give anyone this kind of power over us. The question becomes, when hate is taking away all of our choices and freedoms, what would love do? For myself, love does whatever it can to stop that from happening.

By 5-4 Vote, Supreme Court Lifts Restrictions on Prayer Meetings in Homes

- https://www.nytimes.com/2021/04/10/us/supreme-court-coronavirus-prayer-meetings.html

Time to Stand

I wish that the Covid narrative and vaccine were the only things that we needed to stand up to, but this is far from the case. Unfortunately, of all the things to sound the alarm about, our children are being taught about aberrant sexuality with the most extraordinary silence from parents that the world has ever seen. Nonetheless, the church remains silent as our children are being taught there is no such thing as men or women. On the next page is an actual illustration of what is being shown to kids from kindergarten to the fourth grade.

This kind of curriculum is leading to an epidemic of gender

confusion. In England, between 2018 and 2019, there was a 1,460% increase in referrals for gender dysphoria of boys and a staggering 5,337% increase in girls. However, the fundamental truth is that our children are just children until puberty starts, and that can take up to five years to complete. Talking about sexually related material before this time frame is entirely inappropriate. Unfortunately, our President Joe Biden is talking about gender re-assignment at eight years old.

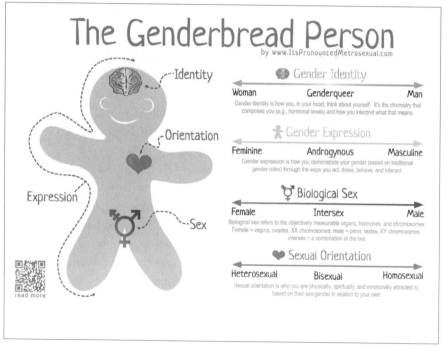

The Genderbread Person
by www.ItsPronouncedMetrosexual.com

Identity

Orientation

Expression

Sex

read more

🌐 Gender Identity

Woman — Genderqueer — Man

Gender identity is how you, in your head, think about yourself. It's the chemistry that composes you (e.g., hormonal levels) and how you interpret what that means.

🧍 Gender Expression

Feminine — Androgynous — Masculine

Gender expression is how you demonstrate your gender (based on traditional gender roles) through the ways you act, dress, behave, and interact.

☿ Biological Sex

Female — Intersex — Male

Biological sex refers to the objectively measurable organs, hormones, and chromosomes. Female = vagina, ovaries, XX chromosomes; male = penis, testes, XY chromosomes; intersex = a combination of the two.

❤ Sexual Orientation

Heterosexual — Bisexual — Homosexual

Sexual orientation is who you are physically, spiritually, and emotionally attracted to, based on their sex/gender in relation to your own.

- https://finance.yahoo.com/news/why-joe-biden-wrong-gender-181000982.html

In early American history, President Franklin D. Roosevelt is pictured wearing a dress. That is because back then they recognized that kids are just kids, and they all wore whatever was convenient, or they could afford. As a result, children were sheltered and protected from worrying whether they were a boy or a girl. Unfortunately, sheltering is not the case today. Instead, the predators have taken over our schools. Teachers teach elementary students about oral sex, masturbation, touching each other's genitals, vaginal intercourse, kissing, grinding, and anal sex.

They show pornographic materials to elementary students, which is illegal according to Section 1466A and 2251 of Title 18, United States Code. One example of this kind of pornographic content is found in the book *It's Perfectly Normal* by Robbie H. Harris and Michael Emberly. The sexual content we are teaching in our schools, movies, and television is producing a massive shift away from the truth. One of my favorite sayings is that we cannot have an epidemic of a genetic disease. Yet, a new epidemic is happening because we have abandoned our children to sin. Suddenly, everyone is being born this way. But, "From the beginning... God made them male and female" (Genesis 5:2).

God is the one who assigns our gender, and He doesn't somehow put us in the wrong bodies. The point is this is what our children are now being taught. If the church cannot stand up to evil even when our little children's souls are at stake, I would say that it is time just to shut the doors and stop pretending we are anything. Nowhere is this pretending happening more than in the church. But in order to stop this, churches would have to work together to make that happen.

Unfortunately, churches can't work together, and they know it. They are unwilling to face their own issues before that can happen. Yet, until pastors begin to love each other and work together, no one is going to believe that Jesus loves anyone. A reformation in the hearts of our pastors has to take place if they are going to work together. If you are interested in joining the movement to protect our children, the following are some excellent resources.

- Protect Our Children Project –
  https://www.pocp.org/about

- Freedom Speaks - https://freedomspeaks.us

- Florida Family Policy Counsel - https://www.flfamily.org

The Divide Is Here

Do not assume that I have come to bring peace to the earth; I have not come to bring peace, but a sword. For I have come to turn a man against his father, a daughter against her mother, a daughter-in-law against her mother-in-law (Matthew 10:34 BSB).

What people forget is that Jesus also came to give the world a choice that they never had before: the hope of glory. Unfortunately, the idea that there is something better called God is still hotly debated. The controversy remains, is there a higher good, and is there something that is "not good enough"? While it is human nature to divide ourselves, this same division is now being enforced with masks, social distancing, and now vaccines carrying genetic components. Indeed, a new kind of racism and segregation has begun with vaccine passports and will one day end with the MOB.

However, the fact that the Covid narrative fits the MOB scenario so well means that the church is capitulating with the MOB plan right now. Mandates to our bodies should be universally resisted even if this isn't the MOB. We have also failed to address bold lies that can be exposed with minimal amounts of investigation. Essentially, recommending people take a vaccine that is not a vaccine is participating in a lie. If we can't say no to a genetic therapy that is just a bad idea, how will we say no to something with much more impact? Indeed, part of being a good parent is to teach your kids when to say no. Teaching us to say no is where our spiritual leaders have failed. We have raised an entire generation of Christians that go along with everything as if that is what Jesus did. Furthermore, few have considered or even heard how the MOB may be the most important part of Satan's plan.

Standing Up to Evil

Of course, the Covid agenda has accomplished many astonishing things that have hurdled us towards a globalist future. If we were to realize the only one thing stopping worldwide communism was America, then how might that help us wake up to what is happening? Because of the Covid narrative, they were able to get mail-in ballots, shut down our whole economy, and get us to spend 15.1 trillion dollars. Pick one bad thing over the past year and a half, and the Covid narrative was how they accomplished it.

When their goal is to destroy America, just look at how far they have gotten in just the past year. We are one more shut down away from all of us being totally dependent on our government. Everyone is acting as if Covid is the only thing that is wrong with the world. Yet, for 1.8% of the money we spent on Covid, we could have saved 36 times as many people due to malaria, hunger, and waterborne illnesses. Election integrity, being able to work, educate our children, maintain our borders, control our national debt, and have freedom of religion have all become unimportant. Once again, this is how the blitzkrieg of chaos has caused us to lose our bearings on what is important in order to execute their final plan.

The War Has Begun

Remember, everything we are struggling with here in America is much worse around the world. We are the world's only material hope, but our real hope is in the Lord. Still, if we will continue to capitulate with something that is the precursor to MOB and causes us to lose our religious freedoms, then what do you think we're going to do with the real thing? We have to realize that our enemy is on the verge of complete control of the world.

Even our Constitution is at stake, but it doesn't matter because they aren't obeying it. Speech and information are already restricted. The church remains one of the only places we can still hear uncensored speech. We also have to stop letting people think we are living in a bubble because everyone is going through the same things. Consequently, we must join the cause of our brothers and sisters around the world in their suffering. When the churches in California were shut down, did all the churches ban together? You already know the answer.

What I am going to say is simple. If something doesn't happen soon, we will lose all our freedoms in the name of peace and safety over an imaginary villain. Based upon the technologies that are currently available, we are close to becoming fish in the barrel. Covid fear has us literally throwing the baby out with the bathwater. But now is the time to wake up. Living with our eyes open is one of the purposes of prophecy, which is the true testimony of Jesus.

The Rockefeller Plan

The Rockefeller Lockstep plan of 2010 is a simulated global outbreak that required steps, various phases, overall timelines, and expected outcomes. While it is difficult to pin down the authenticity of this plan, the problem is that this plan is exactly what is happening right now. Laura Ingraham of *Fox News* covered this report on June 11, 2021. She talked about how eerily similar it is to what is happening with the Covid narrative down to some very fine details. Alex Jones also covered this report (see link below).

When we add this idea to things like Real ID2020, the Georgia Guide Stones, The Great Reset World Economic Forum, and Event 201 Pandemic Exercise, it becomes easier to see the cabal of players behind the conspiracy described in Revelation 18:23. The powerful international merchants and prominent men of the earth are part of Mystery Babylon whose soul goal is to cause the light of God to go out inside of us forever. This is the agenda that we need to stand up to.

- https://www.youtube.com/watch?v=sqiWgpLdm2g

- https://www.warroomforum.com/threads/alex-jones-video-news-laura-ingraham-covers-operation-lockstep-pandemic-lockdown-plan-by-the-rockefeller-foundation.10923/

- https://stateofthenation.co/?p=20234

- https://www.youtube.com/watch?v=AoLw-Q8X174

The Game Is Still Afoot

Fortunately, we still have plenty to fight for, and God is still working through all of this. There are boatloads of people who are not marked, mingled, or sealed on their foreheads either way. So, now is the time to speak out about not taking the MOB and how the only way to be safe is to deny access to our bodies no matter how great their cause. We really could see them release a weapon's grade version of this just to say, "I told you so." Unfortunately, one-third would also be prophetic to one of the plagues of the end times.

Indeed, we were told the deception was going to be great. But most of us have put it off because we were hoping we weren't going to be there. Even now, so many people are hanging on to Trump, but I am hanging onto Jesus. The reality is that Trump did very little to destroy the false Covid narrative. Trump also appointed Fauci, instead of appointing a Covid task force with all the best doctors in the world. These changes alone could have given us a totally different outcome. Trump was also the one who put the emergency order into effect and fast-tracked and promoted a vaccine that doesn't work. Of course, it is also interesting that these supposed vaccines came out days after the election.

Yet, setting up the beast and his mark is their most important agenda. Unfortunately, many Christians are stuck in the paradigm that they cannot lose their salvation, and, in general, I agree with them. But there has never been something like the MOB before. It can do something to us that has never been done before. Once we take it, the gospel no longer affects us. We will not and we cannot repent of our sins for some unknown reason. Maybe the gospel no longer applies to us. Still, the Bible is the only thing that is trustworthy in times like these. We can no longer afford to dumb down the Bible to protect the people from what it says is coming.

Unfortunately, what the Bible says is coming is already here; we just aren't talking about it. People are already in a situation where they are being threatened into taking something they don't need, isn't safe, and doesn't work, or they will lose their job. Even more frightening is that this same system will manipulate them into taking the real MOB, and it will cost them any chance of salvation. The time for mincing words is over. We are seeing these things happening, so let's do what the Bible says, "Stand up, and lift up our heads because our redemption is drawing close" (Luke 21).

What Happened to Prayer and Discernment?

Now is the time for prayer and discernment, not watching more TV. Ask yourself, why haven't you read the Harbinger Part Two? Why was there no massive demonstration of repentance of our sins on Washington Mall? Why isn't Bible prophecy part of the church? Why is it only something that we talk about when things are going bad? Why aren't we clinging to our Bibles? Why aren't we asking God what He is doing and emphatically joining Him?

Remember, proclaiming truth is the proper function of the church, but truth is also the person of Jesus. The spirit of Bible prophecy is proclaiming to the world, "Jesus is still in control." Of course, now is the time to fast, seek the Lord, and ask Him what He is doing. While current events are disturbing, God is also getting ready to do a mighty work inside of all of us in order to bring Jesus to a new generation. Very soon, the hearts of most people will begin to fail them for fear (Luke 21:26).

But no matter what happens, we do not grieve like those who have no hope (1 Thessalonians 4:13). On the contrary, if we began to address what is really on the minds and hearts of the people, then soon we would be able to put out a message of hope like never before. Jesus specifically told us to not, "let not our heart be troubled" because He has prepared a place for us (John 14:1-3). God has told us that all the nations will be shaken (Haggai 2:7). Yet, God caused us to be born for a time like this. Now is the time to go about our Father's business.

One time, while I was writing this book, I became extremely troubled about what was happening. My prayers became more and more intense as I poured out my heart to God. Suddenly, a scripture came to mind. "What is that to you?" (John 21:18-22) I was offended for a moment, but then I realized that I was the guy in that story complaining and not trusting in the sovereignty of God. The next thing I heard was the scripture I just used, "I will shake all the nations." It wasn't long before I realized that the reason God is doing this is to wake us up.

While God is telling us the time is short, God told me to stop playing God and to trust Him. While much of the world will be divided and in travail, we can still lobby for love and truth. Nothing that is happening right now is what love would do. Yet, Jesus told us that this would happen.

> Do not lose heart, because He has overcome the world. Though outwardly we are wasting away, yet inwardly we are renewed day by day. For our light and momentary troubles are achieving us an eternal glory that far outweighs them all. So, we fix our eyes not on what is seen, but what is unseen, since what is seen is temporary, but what is unseen is eternal (2 Corinthians 4:16-18).

What is happening in our country and around the world is supposed to wake us up and help us break away from the world's narratives and approach the throne of God. Unfortunately, America is no longer Christian in any way. Yet, for most people, "All lives still matter," and we must tirelessly represent them. Renewing our minds about what is essential can help people remember who we really are (Romans 12:2). It is reaffirming our identity that helps us guard our heart. Our identity in Christ is what will help us to remember that with Him we can do all things (Philippians 4:13). What we cannot change is what time it is, but what we can change is who we are depending on and worshipping.

An Issue of Trust and Worship

Cursed is the one who trusts in man, who draws strength from mere flesh and whose heart turns away from the LORD (Jeremiah 17:5 NIV).

Like Dr. Zelenko, I want to ask you, whom do we trust for your health, wealth, and well-being? Anything we trust more than God is a false god in our life. How can we think that someone can write better mRNA than God? I get that we want to be helpful, good citizens, but the invasive abuse has started. Not saying anything means we are complicit with the abuser of our freedoms. Most people are bothered by this whole mess, but they figure that if there was something really wrong, their pastor would say something. How is this not the blind leading the blind?

If God is the God of our lives, we can trust in what the Bible says more than we believe in the Covid drama that has swallowed this nation whole. Now is the time to stand up and let our light shine on a different narrative that promotes the truth and represents the lives that don't seem to matter. We must preach that God is still on His throne. Consequently, we will no longer be "tossed to and fro, and carried about with every wind of doctrine, by the sleight of men, and cunning craftiness, whereby they lie in wait to deceive." Now is the time to keep the churches open and to deny mandatory access to our bodies.

While our government and even companies are threatening us, we cannot be afraid of them, and we cannot go along with them any longer (Matthew 10:28). I find it interesting that worship is something we do with our bodies and not just our spirit. Worship is not just about reverence, honor, and respect for everything that God is and does. True worship requires a physical posture towards God. Indeed, the two main words for worship are H7812 in Hebrew and G4352 in Greek, and they mean to bow down, crouch, prostrate, or submit to in obedience.

We Cannot Bend or Bow

What we submit to, obey, or capitulate to is our God. This is the kind of worship that has become lost in our society. But this is exactly what giving someone our right hand represents. Peaceful non-compliance makes sense when we think about Shadrach, Meshach, and Abednego. When the king of Babylon made an image of himself and commanded everyone to worship it, these three young men refused. In the same way, it does not matter what kings and governments are doing around the world; that doesn't change anything for us.

What I have asked myself about this story is how does bending our knee somehow equate to worshiping something? Why didn't they just kneel and still keep worshiping the true God or just pray for forgiveness? But they didn't do that. What did they know that we don't? These three Israelites understood that bending their knees was the same as worship, which means complying with an ungodly mandate is worshiping a false god. Confronting evil is why they stood up, and why we need to stay standing. Indeed, following God is how we survive the fiery furnace that is coming.

Later, Shadrach, Meshach, Abednego, and even Daniel would be right back in trouble when they refused the king's mandate to eat unclean meat sacrificed to false gods. For them, eating this meat was taking something into their body that would defile them.

Likewise, we could also be convicted about not taking these supposed vaccines into our bodies, and this is a legitimate concern, religious or not. Yet the correlation with these Old Testament stories is difficult to miss as we try and broaden our understanding of what it means to worship anything.

Right now, we are being asked to bend the knee, bow our heads, and take something into our bodies that overwrites what God has written. Even if this is only the precursor to the MOB, we are setting up a dangerous precedent. Consequently, standing up to lies with the truth is why we cannot worship, honor, or submit to the beast and his agenda. If Shadrach, Meshach, and Abednego refused to move their bodies into a position of submission or take certain foods into their body, then why can't we refuse to roll up our sleeves and submit our bodies to an agenda that isn't even working on any level?

While we are called to submit to the governing bodies where they have authority (Romans 13:1), we cannot submit in areas where God has spoken (Acts 4:19-20). In this case, God has spoken. We are not to give up access to our bodies just because a great cause appears in the world. We cannot give in to their threats because Christians are not supposed to submit to something that falls within this biblical scenario.

What I am telling us all to do is to submit to God and His Word and follow your conscience! If you have taken this vaccine, please remember, as near as we can tell, it is only a precursor to the MOB. But the time to get off the bandwagon is now. More importantly, we need to join our brothers and sisters in promoting freedom to choose either way. Of course, there really could be some adverse side effects as many are currently experiencing. Unfortunately, only time will tell of the negative side effects. Still, we must remember that our hope is eternal and that God loves a repentant heart.

Therefore, I urge you, brothers, on account of God's mercy, to offer your bodies as living sacrifices, holy and pleasing to God, which is your spiritual service of worship (Romans 12:1 BSB).

Jesus Called Us to Stand Up

Therefore, "Come out from them and be separate, says the Lord. Touch no unclean thing, and I will receive you" (2 Corinthians 6:17 NIV)

As a doctor, I am concerned, and so I am standing up for what I see is a clear and present danger. Essentially, I believe we will continue to see the appearance of Covid variants and even super strains. These variants are happening either through the overuse of supposed vaccines on people who have no risk, or because they are engineered just like they did this one. Meanwhile, according to doctors like Dr. Bauer, we are seeing that our broad range of neutralizing antibodies continue to go down after the jab. In other words, the treatment plan we are on is creating stronger viruses and weaker immune systems. This alone is troubling and could certainly trigger an outbreak of ADE syndrome.

We have seen how the Covid books have been cooked. But now they only consider someone vaccinated between 15 days after their second shot up to three months, which allows them to blame all of the vax deaths and cases upon the un-jabbed. Of course, they still use an inaccurate test that many times doesn't even differentiate between Covid and the flu. To top it all off, it doesn't matter why you went to the hospital or even died. If you tested positive for Covid, then they diagnose and bill your insurance for Covid because the financial incentives are better than anything else.

Furthermore, not only has the media smeared every other form of treatment, now they are smearing natural immunity, which is fundamentally telling us that we can no longer trust God and what He did when He made our body. What is important to realize is

that fear is Covid's only prescription. This is in contrast to what
God has told us, which is that "perfect love casts out fear." This is
important because we have officially entered a time when other
"men's hearts are failing them for fear" (1 John 4:18). Now is the
time to let the world know that hope still lives within us.

God wants us to be distinct from the rest of the world because
we still have the good news that has a way of destroying a lot of
bad news. But if we fail to pass on the truth, people will perish because they have the wrong information. While the road to hell is
paved with the best intentions, the road to heaven is paved with
faith and trust in Jesus, who is the way, the truth (correct information), and the life. While Jesus was the incarnation of love, He
could not capitulate with the lies of the scribes and Pharisees, and
we cannot either. Furthermore, if Jesus always submitted to every
earthly authority, then why did they kill Him?

The fact that they killed Jesus for political reasons seems to escape most of us. Yet, Jesus told us that they would do the same to
some of us (Matthew 24:9). Surely, Jesus was not a mild or meek-
mannered little man because He was not afraid to call out the religious leaders of His day for who they were on the inside. Standing
with Jesus means standing for the truth in these trying times. The
Covid narrative is why we are at a crossroads where truth, submission, and worship all hang in the balance. We have two choices.

We can either believe the biblical narrative or keep trying to fit
into the world's lies. Unfortunately, when we just try and get along,
we may also be going along with the Satanic plan that will eventually land a mark on all of us. In this sense, we have bowed down to
their false image and gone along with a wholesale lie. Yet, the
Covid narrative should send us all a message about just how powerful our adversary is. They have produced one lie after another
and covered them on TV 24/7 until they have manipulated our entire society into giving our pearls to the swine.

God Is Still Working

For the testimony of Jesus is the spirit of prophecy (Revelation 19:10 NKJV)

Now is the time to recall that the spirit of prophecy is encouragement! Take a moment to think about that. How is this encouraging? Because God wants us to know that He knew all of this was going to happen. God knows the big picture. If God knows the big picture and the future, then God knows our future, and we can trust Him with our very lives. While there is some immediacy to the situations we are now facing, now is the time to remove our anger and strengthen our resolve.

We still have hope, and that hope is not just something to be had in the future. God is offering us a better relationship with Him now than we have ever had before. In other words, there is a substance to our faith and our hope. Once again, while this book has focused on what Satan is doing, we do not want to end without giving honor to what God is still doing in the world. Most importantly, as you read these words, God is saying that you have a key part to play in this divine drama that will be remembered for all eternity. Yet, we are at a tipping point.

Now is the time to say enough is enough. Not in a way that causes division or hate, but one that sheds light on the truth. Unfortunately, we can only know our part if we focus on what we have so often refused, which is a deeper relationship with God. God is calling His people to Himself because He will use our voice to reach the world. With all that has been said, I pray that you will hear your script, straight from the throne of God, and may it come welling up inside you, so that we can all say together, "Thy will be done on earth as it is in heaven."

Fear of man will prove to be a snare, but whoever trusts in the Lord is kept safe (Proverbs 29:25 NIV).

What I am calling for is a time of prophetic awakening for us to realize what time it is—a time when we fully invest ourselves in God's kingdom. Consequently, we must pick a godly fight and fight it in a godly way. Indeed, it is through faith we recognize that God's kingdom is within us, so we cannot ultimately lose. Still, we must stand on the side of truth, personal freedoms, religious freedoms, and against tyranny of any kind. But this is the point that we have to admit to ourselves that things will not go back to normal. Satan is in control of all the key players.

The only thing left is the pulpits of our churches and the space found in our living rooms. We are no longer living in peacetime. Consequently, we are about to find out who are the real soldiers. We need men of courage because the bullets are already flying. People are being hurt. Unfortunately, merely talking a big game is not going to work. If we don't fight for our freedoms, then we won't have them. Either we turn this country around through prayer, repentance, dedication, and a pouring out of God's Spirit, or we are headed towards a total loss of freedom.

I like to remind people that the communists have always said that they would take over our country without ever firing a shot, which may be coming true. Unfortunately, history shows that they kill the prophets because they stood at the crossroads issuing a warning very few heeded. Warning! There is a new kind of worship that is coming. Shadrach, Meshach, and Abednego refused to worship a false god, and it all came down to something as small as bending their knees or refusing to take something unholy into their body. Consequently, I believe we need to be aware of a new kind of worship founded in disobedience and capitulation.

For Jesus to glorify His Father, He had to submit His body to God. He had to open up His arms and consent to the cross. Trust was how Jesus became obedient even unto death. Who we worship is about who we obey, trust, comply with, go along with, and allow access to our bodies. Understanding other biblical standards of worship can easily explain why we cannot roll up our sleeves for a false narrative of fear. The only fear worth anything is the fear of the Lord, and it is the beginning of wisdom.

Submission or allowing access to our temples of the Holy Spirit is exactly how taking the MOB is worshiping Satan. The question is, are you and the people you love prepared to say no? Is the church ready to take its place and stand against this deception, or will it make peace with the devil? My prayer is that we wake up the sleeping virgins, be the salt in light of the decay, and occupy until He comes. It does not matter that our enemy has come, because the Lord will also come in like a flood, and raise up a standard against him (Isaiah 59:19).

Lastly, when we have made peace with God to the point that we know He "will never leave us, or forsake us," we will be able to join the saints and say with full confidence, "The Lord is my helper; I will not be afraid. What can man do to me?" (Hebrews 13:5-6) Even now, God is ready to send a new kind of prophet into the world—one that is as wise as a serpent and harmless as a dove. May God bless you as you grow ever closer to Him. May we also pay close attention to our walk, "redeeming the time, because the days are evil" (Ephesians 5:16).

Behold, I am sending you out like sheep among wolves; therefore, be as shrewd (wise) as snakes and as innocent [harmless] as doves (Matthew 10:16 BSB).

Last Minute Update
Still Cooking the Books

So much has happened since finishing my original manuscript that I felt compelled to write a few last-minute updates. Cooking the books is alive and well. Whenever someone goes to the hospital, they are given a Covid test. If they test positive, they are diagnosed with Covid regardless of whether they have had a car accident or heart attack. Why? All because of the financial incentives. Of course, if they die, they also die of Covid, thereby inflating the numbers. As we have covered, the test for Covid-19 is inaccurate and can easily be rigged if it is cycled too many times.

Furthermore, many Covid tests do not differentiate between Covid and the flu.[1] Indeed, with rules like these, they can manufacture a perpetual pandemic. Considering that over half of hospitalizations test positive upon admission,[2] we should not be surprised that 50% of COVID hospitalizations have mild symptoms or are asymptomatic.[3] Either of these statistics reveal that the number of hospitalizations is meaningless. One of the most egregious exaggerations of the Covid numbers came when the *New York Times* had to issue a correction concerning child hospitalizations from August 2020 to October 2021. How far off were they? They only inflated the numbers from 63,000 to 900,000!

Effectively, they misled and bullied millions of Americans into needlessly jabbing their children, even though the skyrocketing cases of myocarditis in these same children were well documented. But, statistics like these are only part of the cover-up. A 5/1/21 decision by the CDC to only track breakthrough infections of the unvaccinated not only furthered their false narrative about the success of the jab, but retriggered a surge in cases because the vaccinated falsely believed they were immune.[4]

However, if we do not keep statistics on both groups equally, we cannot say that the jab is a success. But blaming the unvaccinated and minimizing vaccine deaths is the name of the game. For instance, no one is considered vaccinated until 15 days after their second shot, and then only three months.[5] Recalling that 50% of the deaths recorded on VAERS happen in 24 hours and 80% in the first week, we can see how they intentionally hide the vaccine injuries. Yet, when we factor in that VAERS only represents 1-10% of the total adverse events, we could have 150,000 to 1.5 million deaths from the jab.

[1] https://www.foxnews.com/health/cdc-labs-covid-tests-differentiate-flu/

[2] https://www.telegraph.co.uk/news/2021/07/26/exclusive-half-covid-hospitalisations-tested-positive-admission/

[3] https://www.theatlantic.com/health/archive/2021/09/covid-hospitalization-numbers-can-be-misleading/620062/?utm_source=facebook&utm_medium=social&utm_campaign=share&fbclid=IwAR39vBbK0CCYzUjaVeL15IiasZkw27U_eXHmekzJaP8LD4sS1VwePu9gJY/

[4] https://www.msn.com/en-us/news/us/the-cdc-only-tracks-a-fraction-of-breakthrough-covid-19-infections-even-as-cases-surge/ar-AANzQbl/

[5] https://www.bitchute.com/video/P81FKY43pI7Q/

Fortunately, parts of the world are starting to see the truth. Sweden, Denmark, and Finland have all banned Moderna's vaccine in people under 30, but Iceland went further and eliminated Moderna completely.[6] Still, people keep drinking the Kool-Aid. Even though we were told these jabs were 90%+ effective or that Biden would never issue a vaccine mandate, it hasn't made Americans wake up or realize they have been lied to. It doesn't even seem to matter that the NIH agrees that Fauci was lying about "gain of function" research at Wuhan.[7]

It gets worse. In a town hall meeting on 10/21/21, Biden went on to call the un-jabbed murderers, even though the jabbed can catch and spread Covid like anyone else. "Freedom? I have the freedom to kill you with my Covid?" (Picture loud applause) But if the jabbed are less symptomatic, they are the ones who are more likely spreading Covid. More importantly, when President Biden blocked Florida Governor Ron Desantos from obtaining life-saving Regeneron (monoclonal antibody) treatments for his state, he expressed his freedom to murder people with his political agenda. Yet, where is the outrage for these blatant lies, and why has it become un-Christian to call them out? But is continuing to re-main silent what Jesus would do?

The Vaccines Have Failed

Multiple sources have entirely ruled out that we can obtain herd immunity from the vaccine. According to Sir Andrew Pollard (Professor of Pediatric Infection and Immunity at the University of Oxford),[8] Þórólfur Guðnason (Icelandic doctor and the Chief Epidemiologist of the Icelandic Directorate of Health),[9] and Dr. Hans Kluge (World Health Organization Regional Director for Europe), the vaccine has failed.[10] The only path forward is natural immunity. Dr. Pollard went on to suggest that "the next thing may be a variant which is perhaps even better at transmitting in vacci-nated populations."

In a definitive statement regarding the failure of the jab, the European Journal of Epidemiology studied 68 countries and 2947 counties in the United States and found that increases in COVID-19 are unrelated to levels of vaccination. But Biden still accuses the unjabbed of murder, even though the CDC recently admitted on 9/2/21 that no one with natural immunity has ever spread Covid-19. Thankfully, the world is starting to wake up to this crime against humanity.

For example, a group of world physicians has put forth the

"Rome Declaration," which affirms that the Covid narrative violates their Hippocratic Oath due to wholesale censorship and the outright withholding of life-saving treatments. Some of the most well-known doctors in the world have signed it, including Dr. Robert Malone (inventor of the mRNA vaccine) and Dr. Geert Vanden Bosch.

[6]https://www.westernjournal.com/denmark-sweden-halt-use-moderna-covid-vaccine-everyone-30/?utm_source=Facebook&utm_medium=PostTopSharingButtons&utm_campaign=websitesharingbuttons&fbclid=IwAR1T0CljpsO17oUJP34SSVc8EL7edpF5DrBSLAFAVJPqwaNu7hkhQKjd-8o/

[7]https://trendingpolitics.com/told-you-so-rand-paul-does-victory-lap-after-nih-proves-fauci-was-lying/

[8]https://worldnewsera.com/news/uk/delta-variant-has-ruined-hopes-of-herd-immunity-experts-say/

[9]https://heartlanddaily.com/iceland-herd-immunity-must-be-achieved-by-transmitting-the-virus/?fbclid=IwAR0Q-KiSZXR7epm8M9Jbe9iwA2AxxW5p2-HApEDFEa65zVoPH4kUiQZ_zHo/

[10]https://www.dailymail.co.uk/news/article-9978071/Covid-vaccines-wont-end-pandemic-officials-gradually-adapt-strategy.html/

Nefarious Ingredients

For some time, I have heard about the disturbing ingredients inside the Covid jabs. Seeing someone's hands light up under fluorescence has a way of changing my idea about how close we are to being injected with Luciferase.[11] Next, Dr. Robert Young confirmed the presence of graphene oxide in all of the jabs.[12] Unfortunately, graphene is poisonous to the body, but it does explain why most of my jabbed patients have become magnetic.[13] So, what is graphene's purpose?[1] Graphene oxide can be used for energy production/ storage, +polarity, frequency amplification, and construction of nanobots (i.e., Darpa Hydrogel). Of course, nanobots need to connect to the internet. Could this be the reason behind the push for 5G?

Next, Dr. Carrie Madej discovered some horrific findings in the vaccines.[14] Not only did she see structures similar to graphene, but she saw something assembling itself into a hydra-like creature. Dr. Zandre Botha was also shocked by what she found when studying the blood of her seriously ill vaccinated patients.[15] Dr. Botha observed blood cell stacking and black inanimate objects consistent with graphene. On a dried blood sample with no coverslip, she found a moving grid of black washer-type structures. They appeared to self-assemble and connect.

On Stew Peter's show, Stew interviewed the wife of a soldier forced to take the jab.[16] After falling ill to the jab, he tried to detoxify in a magnetic clay bath. But soon, he felt like he was being stuck with needles. Under a black light, his wife could see these black things poking out of him, so she pulled one out. They looked like tiny moving metal strings, but they appeared to want to get back into his body.

Additionally, Dr. Jane Ruby reviewed the findings of the German physician Dr. Barbel Gitala.[17] Dr. Gitala presented 100s of slides showing dark inanimate objects and blood cells clumping together like coins, which is indicative of blood cancer or Rouleaux that commonly lead to thrombosis and clotting.

[11]https://www.bitchute.com/video/cjRoIf8Q9nD7/& https://www.alecsatin.com/what-is-luciferase/

[12]https://www.bitchute.com/video/zrqm4smKJime/ & https://www.drrobertyoung.com/post/transmission-electron-microscopy-reveals-graphene-oxide-in-cov-19-vaccines/

[13]https://rightsfreedoms.wordpress.com/2021/06/21/study-on-the-electromagnetism-of-vaccinated-persons-in-lux-embourg/

[14]https://www.redvoicemedia.com/2021/09/dr-carrie-madej-first-u-s-lab-examines-vaccine-vials-horrific-find-ings-revealed/

[15]https://www.redvoicemedia.com/2021/10/never-before-seen-blood-doctor-reveals-horrific-findings-after-exam-ining-vials/

[16]https://www.redvoicemedia.com/2021/10/stew-peters-show-vaxxed-soldier-detox-horrific-video-peter-navarro-live-vaxx-vials-breaking-update-and-more/

[17]https://thetruedefender.com/watch-german-physicians-reveal-horrific-findings-in-the-blood-of-vaxxed-patients/

Dr. Gitala and Dr. Bolland also reviewed a vial of the J&J jab, which revealed rigid structures and tiny dots that would later form a lattice-type structure.[18] They had never seen them before. After gathering a few doctors and lawyers, they were still afraid to go public. Of particular concern was finding a judge to hear the case, much less go against it.

Pfizer whistleblower Karen Kingston has also gone on record talking about the existing patents of what these doctors have found. Specifically, the entity that looks like what Dr. Botha observed is US patent #2010/0216804 A1 and is described as long circular nanoparticles capable of targeting specific parts of the body for delivery of drugs, gene therapies, toxic immune therapies, or medical diagnosis. But the patent is also adamant in saying the invention is "not limited to only what is described here."

Karen also reveals that Moderna's mRNA vaccine patent can be used for a "sustained release of compounds/biological agents" from hours to years, which means what they have put inside of us may not even be turned on yet. Essentially, Ms. Kingston believes this is an "obedience training program." She elaborates by talking about the G2G Go program in Australia pairs devices in our bodies with our phones to track location, push notifications, require check-ins, and administer treatments based upon an individual's risk calculations.

Failure to comply can lead to fines of up to $50,000 or imprisonment. Karen also explains why they are not giving informed consent for the jab. According to Public Law 114–255 on 12/13/16, section 3024, given an Emergency Use Order (EUA) or clinical research, informed consent can be waived if it is deemed not in our best interest to know. But this is a clear violation of international law. If nanotechnologies can be legally placed inside our bodies without our permission, the possibilities for abuse are endless. Nanobots can diagnose, treat, reward, punish, change our DNA, or terminate us. There would be no need for the police. Now we know what Tal Zaks meant when he referred to the jab as an "operating system."

The "final end game" starts to come into view with the discoveries of Dr. Frank Zalewski, who also released pictures of what he calls the "Thing."[19] Indeed, Dr. Zalewski believes the jab is a "stealth insertion of self-replicating synthetic biology lifeforms" in the form of eggs, which grow, multiply and hatch in the presence of graphene. Dr. Zalewski also believes the COVID test swabs are being used to create a DNA database. So, what else does he think this is? "Transhumanism through a parasite... a fancy new lifeform concocted in a military lab, and proliferating inside human bodies, mixing its DNA with ours, replacing it, destroying it... who knows?" Then he says, "This world, we have to realize, is almost lost." Stew on that a minute.

But there is still something missing. None of these technologies work without a sophisticated AI "operating system" that links them together. Enter Lynn Parker, the director of the National Artificial Intelligence Initiative. Lynn has already declared her intent to "fill the AI talent gap" and "prepare US workers" for this future. Maybe this is why they are firing people and creating shortages to create openings for the robot workforce. On 1/25/21, *Reuters News* declared, "Makers of Sophia the robot plan mass rollout amid pandemic." Of course, the name Sophia (the highest god in Gnosticism) has now been changed to "Grace."

[18]https://ugetube.com/watch/karen-kingston-receipts-for-cyrus-parsa-039-s-wild-a-i-claims-stew-peters-show_drtXJzTTnN6J6Bv.html/ & https://www.redvoicemedia.com/2021/10/receipts-patent-proves-vaxx-is-obedience-training-platform-the-final-variant/

[19]https://everydayconcerned.net/2021/10/11/more-sickening-covid-vaccine-findings-dr-franc-zalewski-finds-aluminium-lifeform-tentacled-parasite-in-pfizer-vaccine-vaccine-parasites-found-in-vaccinated-blood-causing-blood-clots-heart-iss/

It is important to note that there appear to be some variations in the vaccines and the batches. Some vials may contain nothing, while others have graphene or some unknown creature. Regardless, it is time to consider the possibility that these jabs could be closer to the real MOB than we first thought. Once these things are inside us, all they have to do is add the ingredients, and Satan's kingdom will build itself inside us. Now they are even talking about putting mRNA in our foods and all the other vaccines. The new wave of jabs is even advertising that they change our DNA. In summation, the "final end game" that we have laid out here is how all these pieces can work together to alter the nature of humanity forever and create a "hive mind." Could this "operating system" inside of us explain how the whole world ends up worshiping the beast?

A Day with the Experts

On 11/20/21, I attended "A Day With The Experts Covid-19 Conference" in Tampa Bay, Florida. I heard Dr. Robert Malone, Dr. Peter McCullough, Dr. Carrie Madej, Dr. Sherri Tenpenny, and several other wonderful doctors/attorneys talk about the Covid deception and the dangers of the supposed vaccine. Some of the most globally vilified and published physicians have personally experienced persecution because they have dared to challenge the Covid narrative. Meanwhile, the most significant protests in history are still taking place. Yet, none of these protests ever make it on the news. Unfortunately, most of the world has already lost the battle for their temple, but America is still deciding.

It was prophetic that both Dr. Malone and Dr. McCullough, who may not be Christians or trained in Bible prophecy, called this global entity "the Beast." Dr. Malone also called this our "golden calf." Essentially, this is the false god we have chosen to worship instead of the real God. Even more shocking is that very few ministers have dared to utter such words, which is why Dr. Tenpenny feels that "the church has failed us." This sentiment was shared by several Scientologists that I was witnessing to. "Christians were supposed to protect us from this."

Immediately I got chills because I knew they were both was right. But the sad truth is the church, just like in Nazi Germany, has gone along with the narrative by shutting their doors and taking money to hold vaccine drives on their campuses. Why? Is this escapism? Are they deceived or asleep? Unfortunately, Christians have been told we won't be around for anything bad for so long that they don't know what to do. I don't understand why people are obsessed with the idea of not being here. In fact, I know some people who even wish they could stay and be a witness to those who are left behind. But that idea is one I am still having trouble embracing. Either way, the church's capitulation with the lies of the beast is why we need wholesale repentance if we are ever going to turn back this evil.

For the record, I did not hear one thing at the conference that made me question anything I have said in this book. Therefore, I am doubling down on the idea that this jab is at least the precursor to the MOB. More importantly, I am fully convinced that this co-ordinated worldwide movement to get mandatory access to our bodies is the "beast government" the Bible warned us about. Surely, if we do not stop them now, this great experiment in human freedom will soon be over. I will end with the same admonition Dr. David Jeramiah (and essentially every doctor at the Expert Conference) used when he spoke last month here in Tampa. "Resist in any way we can." May God help us to join together and stay standing until He comes.

Don't you know that when you offer yourselves to someone as obedient slaves, you are slaves of the one you obey? (Romans 6:16 NIV)

Have nothing to do with fruitless deeds of darkness, but rather expose them... Everything exposed by the light becomes visible—that is why it is said: "Wake up, sleeper, rise from the dead, and Christ will shine on you." Be careful then how you live, not as unwise but as wise, making the most of every opportunity because the days are evil (Ephesians 5:1-15 NIV).

About the Author

Dr. Kruse has been practicing Chiropractic in Brandon, Florida, since 1992. However, teaching Bible prophecy has always been his passion. Dr. Kevan is also proud to serve as the president of the board for soilministries.org, a pipeline of vision and resources to Honduras. Dr. Kevan also founded prophecydays.com, and the "Supernatural Junkies" podcast on *Charisma* magazine, which covers all the subjects that are "off limits" in church.

You may contact the author at: info@supernaturaljunkies.com